T0266933

LEAD TOGETHER

STOP SQUIRRELING AWAY POWER
AND BUILD A BETTER TEAM

BY TANIA LUNA

PEAKPOINT
— PRESS —

Peakpoint Press books may be purchased in bulk at special discounts for sales promotion, corporate gifts, fund-raising, or educational purposes. Special editions can also be created to specifications. For details, contact the Special Sales Department, Skyhorse Publishing, 307 West 36th Street, 11th Floor, New York, NY 10018 or info@skyhorsepublishing.com.

Peakpoint® and Peakpoint Press are registered trademarks of Skyhorse Publishing, Inc.®, a Delaware corporation.

Visit our website at www.skyhorsepublishing.com.

10 9 8 7 6 5 4 3 2 1

Cover design by Brian Peterson
Interior illustrations by Process Grey

ISBN: 978-1-5107-7646-3
Ebook ISBN: 978-1-5107-7648-7

Printed in the United States of America

To Ami, my with *everything.*

It seems to me that whereas power usually means power-over, the power of some person or group over some other person or group, it is possible to develop the conception of power-with, *a jointly developed power, a co-active, not a coercive power.*

—Mary Parker Follett (1868–1933)

The creation of a thousand forests is in one acorn.

—Ralph Waldo Emerson

··· Contents ···

PART IV: PRINCIPLES IN ACTION

INTRODUCTION

You are about to go on a strange and important adventure.

Sometimes you will feel like you're reading a business book, full of practical tactics to increase the effectiveness, energy, and adaptivity of those around you. A handbook for preventing burnout, bias, bottlenecks, and conventional thinking. A blueprint for building an unstoppable team. A guide to becoming the kind of leader who makes every person you meet a little better. Other times you will feel like you're reading a novel, full of twists, turns, and peculiar characters who help you see reality in a new light. Sometimes your mind will race ahead with plans for real-life application. Sometimes, you'll get lost in self-reflection, wondering who you are as a leader (and a person) and who you want to become. You might try to tell the people in your life what you're reading and how it's affecting you and struggle to explain just what kind of book it is.

"It's about sharing power as a way to build stronger, more resilient teams," you'll say, and they will nod with interest and perhaps even approval. But then you'll add, "as told through a story about squirrels . . ." And their eyes will widen. "In the workplace," you'll add. And their head will tilt to the side. They'll ask if it's one of those cute business parables. "It's more like philosophical fiction," you'll say, "with practical applications."

"For squirrels?" they might ask, if they're the snarky type.

"For everyone," you'll answer.

Sometimes you'll wish this book took a more conventional approach, simply laying out all the tactics for you to collect and apply.

You'll find periodic summaries and check-in questions to help you *paws* and transfer insights back into your life (along with an abundance of squirrel puns I hope you won't *critter-size* me for over-using). You can access bonus tools, resources, and a community of values-aligned people at www.TaniaLuna.com. You'll also get a comprehensive guide to all the ideas in the book, but not until the end, once you've completed your journey. That's because ideas do their best work through story.[1] Ideas are most powerful and beautiful not as plucked flowers dropped into a pretty vase but as seeds buried in the soil of our minds, where they grow into wild things native to their land. We might never know how squirrels' minds work, but we know ideas seeds are at the root of how we humans learn and how we make ideas stronger—not by being told what to think but by having the power to come to our own conclusions.

Now as for the ideas in this book . . . You'll find that many of them feel timely, even urgent. You'll recognize that our deepest struggles at work, in society, and across our planet today have to do with poor power distribution. You'll see that it's our greatest vulnerability, especially in the midst of change and uncertainty. You'll diagnose it as the glaring cause of stress, distrust, and disengagement, not just among those who have too little power but also those who hold too much—those lonely leaders who long for a team to lift the weight of the world off their shoulders. You'll realize our relationship to power is fundamentally broken and needs repair. And you'll discover how to use your own power to mend this relationship and build a more fair, fulfilling, and flourishing world within and outside the workplace.

Many of these ideas may feel fresh, but they have been growing for a long time under the care of many wise gardeners. Some of these individuals and their insights will make appearances in the book. Rest assured any research they mention is based on actual scientific findings with human, rather than squirrel, participants. For research citations see the Notes section. For a full cast of characters and the people who inspired them, turn to the Inspiration section following the story.

Chief among these characters is a brilliant thinker and writer named Mary Parker Follett, who lived between 1868 and 1933 and thoroughly stirred up business culture with her power-with philosophy. She was highly influential in her time, yet, despite several efforts to bring her into modern consciousness, she and her thinking have been mostly lost to us. Perhaps this time we're ready to listen, and her ideas will finally break through.

Before a wise friend of mine introduced me to Mary Parker Follett's writing, I came to many of the same conclusions via my personal experience, eight decades after Follett's time. Without realizing it, my coworkers and I turned our company, LifeLabs Learning, into a practice lab for sharing power in the workplace. We implemented each of the tactics in this book and reaped the rewards. Throughout my tenure as co-CEO, not only did we help roughly two thousand companies become richly collaborative and fulfilling places to work, but we also grew our own organization from the ground up to over $30 million in revenue, 150 employees, 96 percent employee engagement, and less than 2 percent attrition, without outside funding and even through a pandemic. Most rewarding of all, we became the kind of community that continues to make each other better.

At my current company, Scarlet Spark, we help leaders in the animal protection movement thoughtfully share their power to create organizational-level and world-level change. In the meantime, we experiment on ourselves so we can keep discovering new ways to amplify each other's power. In short, none of the ideas woven into this book exist in the realm of theory (or squirrels). Every single one is backed by a combination of academic research and lived experience.

But the most important ideas all along this adventure will be your own. These are ideas that will help you understand the nature of power at work and in life. These are ideas that will help you lead not from the front or from behind, but to lead together. These are ideas that will make you a more powerful leader and person. That, in and of itself, is a worthwhile outcome. But it's only the first step. The next is to ask yourself, *How will I use my power?*

In a moment, you will meet Sam, the hero of our story. You'll get to see the world through his eyes and meet the individuals in his life. Sure, they all happen to be squirrels, but see if you can find your own story reflected in his.

Will you recognize people you know in Sam or in his coworkers? Will any of the pressures on his little squirrel shoulders mirror the pressures you carry on your human ones? In what ways is your leadership philosophy similar to his, and in what ways is it different?

Let's turn the page and find out.

PART I

SAM THE SQUIRREL

Chapter 1

An Almost Definitely Great Leader

Sam Squirrel was almost definitely a great leader—at least according to himself. He gathered more nuts than anyone else in the history of Nuts for You, Inc. And he was promoted again and again until he worked his way up to a glamorous treetop office and the title of executive branch manager. In the three months since he leaped into this new role, TNG (total nuts gathered) increased by 20 percent. Now Sam was determined to make his division the most productive acorn-gathering operation in the entire forest. The name Sam would be forever synonymous with *success*. He'd make his boss proud. He'd make his wife proud. And—most important of all—he'd make their two little squirrel pups proud.

"Wow," said Sylvio when Sam mentioned his branch's performance at a meeting of the High Tails, a nut-working group of leaders from local companies. Sylvio was the VP of sales at a nest construction company that seemed to grow perpetually in reverse. He had a glint in his eye that could have been admiration or envy—or maybe a bit of both.

Their small group sat in a circle beneath a willow tree whose long branches swept the ground and curtained them off from the rest of the forest. When they slipped into the cool shade of this secret suite, the usual hum and buzz outside dissolved behind them, and all their chests puffed up ever so slightly. Though today, everyone but Sam seemed more worn down than puffed up. Sylvio looked especially rumpled. His fur stuck up in all directions like he had accidentally foraged a battery.

"You must have one solid team under you," he said, and the other executives nodded.

"I wish," said Sam, and he casually smoothed down his already smooth gray coat, "but these squirrels are half as productive as I was when I was in their position. They don't seem to do anything until I give them direction. But what can I do? There's a talent shortage out there."

"Tell me about it," sighed Eva, the leader of a nut-transportation company. "All these squirrels are moving out of the forest. They say they can't keep working for peanuts, but we can't compete with city salaries."

"And the squirrels who do stay act like they're doing us a favor," said Sylvio.

"Squirrels these days," Eva sighed again.

"Okay, okay, so how'd you do it?" asked Jose, the owner of a nut-counting firm and the most practical squirrel of the group. "How'd you get a 20 percent bump in the middle of the most competitive foraging season?"

All the squirrels leaned in. Jose's tail flinched in anticipation. Sam took a nice long breath and savored the sensation of all those little black eyes turning to him.

"Simple," he said.

"Simple?" Jose demanded.

"You've got to know the way and make them go your way," said Sam.

This was the advice Sam had heard from his boss more times than he could count. He briefly considered crediting him for these words of leadership wisdom but dismissed the thought. This was his moment and his personal philosophy too. He sat back and crossed his sleek, gray-coated arms.

Later that day, as Sam climbed back up the towering oak tree to his office, he replayed the conversation in his head and felt pretty darn proud of himself. The hush that fell over the group amid the soft rustling of willow leaves. All their eyes on him. The glow that spread through his body like warm maple sap. Here he was, succeeding—no, winning—even though he faced the same obstacles that stumped his peers. He knew the way to succeed, and he'd make sure every squirrel at his branch fell in line with his vision. There was almost no doubt about it. He was a great leader.

Sam looked forward to a peaceful rest of the day counting and recounting his branch's reserves, the glorious stash of nuts in his office safe. He would set company-wide priorities for the quarter and maybe even the year. He'd revise the branch's branding all on his own because the marketing department couldn't seem to comprehend the concept of a deadline. And he'd practice his look of genuine surprise when his boss finally named Sam the company's new (and youngest ever) chief nut officer. It wasn't a sure thing yet, but his boss had been dropping hints.

He was so caught up in these pleasant contemplations, he didn't bother to look where he was climbing. When he finally glanced up and saw three bushy tails hanging out of his office doorway, he got so startled he lost his grip on the bark and fell.

CHECK-IN QUESTIONS: LEADERSHIP

Sam's pretty sure he's a great leader. How about you? Jot down your answers here:

- *How do you hope people will describe you as a leader one day?*

- *What are your leadership strengths?*

- *What are your leadership gaps or areas for improvement?*

Chapter 2

The Condo Development

Sam caught a small branch just in time to stop his plummet. Even more important, he turned his yelp into a yell, deftly avoiding a close call with vulnerability.

"Hey!" he shouted. "What are you doing in my office?"

"I'm so sorry, Sam," said Mila, the marketing manager. She stared down at him, clutching her gray tail and looking like she might burst into tears at any moment.

"We have some bad news," said Francesca, the finance manager. Her typically sleek dark gray coat stood up like she had run through a wind tunnel.

Francesca turned to Ravi, the SR (squirrel resources) manager. His patchy fur looked even patchier, with the fur on top of his head almost entirely gone. Ravi caught the glance from Francesca and promptly shot it back to Mila. Mila threw a pleading look back to Francesca.

By now Sam had scurried up into his office and behind his broad oak desk where he sat watching this game of invisible hot potato with growing impatience. This was his management team, the supposed leaders of the branch with which his boss had entrusted him. It really was a wonder he got anything accomplished with them around.

"What's the news?" he asked.

"Condo!" said Mila. And Francesca and Ravi looked down at their feet.

"Condo?"

"Condo," Mila repeated, as though it explained everything. Another long pause.

"Just tell him what you learned," Francesca whispered to Ravi, who winced at the prompt and scratched at a bald patch on his shoulder.

"Okay," said Ravi, "but this isn't coming from me. I found out about it through an exit interview with someone from Research and Development."

"Fine," said Sam. "I don't care who it's coming from as long as it gets here."

"Okay," Ravi continued, still looking down, "it's just that it's not in my job description. And it's a sensitive topic. And really something that should stay between us or on a need-to-know basis, though eventually everyone will know. But for now, as far as I know, only we know."

"Just tell me," Sam said through gritted teeth.

"There's a condo development going up in our forest!" Mila said. Then she shut her eyes tightly as if that would keep the future away and maybe Sam too.

"We crunched some numbers this morning, and it's not good," said Francesca.

"It's very bad," added Mila, folding and unfolding her tail in her paws.

"If they cut down as many trees as we're projecting, we expect a shrink of 80 percent in our Total Available Nuts," said Francesca.

"Eighty percent," Sam repeated, and the three squirrels before him nodded. "That's not enough to feed the families in this forest let alone keep our business alive."

His mind flashed to his two pups in their cozy nest, waiting for him to come home with stories of his day. Francesca finally slicked down her dark gray coat and pulled her shoulders back. No one had seen her look so disheveled for this long, and it seemed she wasn't about to let this slip in her polish continue.

"I'd have to rerun the numbers," she said with regained poise, "but it appears so, yes."

Ravi let out a long sigh. Mila said nothing, but a tiny tear finally broke through her attempts at professionalism and streamed down her furry cheek. Sam closed his eyes and got the distinct feeling he'd lost his grip and was plummeting down from the tree all over again.

CHECK-IN QUESTIONS:
YOUR CHALLENGES

Now that you know Sam's problem, let's talk about yours. What is your version of an endangered forest? What challenges, obstacles, or fears loom over your horizon? Jot them down here so you can benefit more from Sam's struggles, and apply the lessons he learns to your own situation.

Chapter 3

· · · · · · ·

Amara and the Pups

Sam stayed at work for a long time. He seemed unable to get up from his desk, let alone make the commute back home. He resigned himself to spending the night in his office, a practice his wife, Amara, discouraged but tolerated. Sam figured it was for the best. This way, she and the kids could enjoy their blissful ignorance about the condo development just a little while longer. But what would he tell Amara when the time came?

The bright, vivid future he could almost touch just moments ago now seemed as far out of reach as the moon. There would be no promotion, no glowing praise from his boss. And it was unthinkable, but he gave himself permission to think it: *Could he actually lose his job? Could the entire company go under?* From his office window, Sam watched the sky turn deep blue, then violet, then the red of a blood orange. He heard bird song give way to cricket song. But what finally made him shoot up to his feet was a sudden cold flash of memory: he'd promised to tuck in the twins tonight while Amara worked the late shift at her clinic. Now the time to have kept his promise had come and gone.

Amara was the most sought-after dentist in the forest and wanted to keep it that way. She was fond of reminding Sam that squirrels' teeth never stop growing, so neither should her career. They were in constant negotiations over whose work was more post-ponable. But that morning, there had been no battle necessary. Sam assured Amara he'd be home in time to put the pups to bed, not because his work was less important but because he was a great dele-gator. She gave him one of those wry smirks that had made him fall in love with her. She wrapped her soft orange-gray tail around him, the same exact shade as their pups, and gave him a kiss goodbye. Now it felt like years had passed since that morning.

Sam leaped out of his office and made his way down the tree in record time. He darted down the path to his home as his mind raced with excuses—no, explanations for his broken promise to Amara. By the time he reached his home, a beautiful, human handmade squir-rel house that had been in his family for generations, he was brim-ming with righteous indignation in response to all the complaints he imagined he'd hear from his wife and kids. Didn't they know he was the victim here—or better yet, the bruised and battered hero?

He prepared these excellent retorts and many more, but when he squeezed through the hole into his house, all that greeted him on the other side was silence. He didn't think it could be possible to feel sorrier for himself than he already felt, but as he sank to his knees onto the empty nest, he discovered a whole new low. He was about to maybe, possibly cry a little—a practice he generally dis-couraged in himself and others—but then a small, sweet voice rang out behind him.

"Dad!" And then another:

"Dad! Dad!"

Sam spun around to see two tiny black noses poking in through their circle of a doorway. He hopped up to his feet, but the twins flew through the door like little orange whirlwinds and pinned him back down on the nest. The pine house filled with their giggles.

"Dad! Dad!" said Josie. "Mom took us to the clinic with her, and it was so cool and gross."

"Yeah, totally gross and totally cool," said her brother, Remi.

"And everyone said Mom is such a great boss and the best dentist ever," said Josie.

"Yeah, the best anywhere!" said Remi.

The twins bounced on Sam's stomach and flitted around the house with the energy of chipmunks. Sam got so caught up in their giddiness that when he saw Amara's face in the doorway, it felt like an icicle crashed down on his head.

"Excuse me, kiddos," Sam said. Still looking at his wife, he gently lifted one of the pups' tails off his forehead and patted another twin on the head. He crawled outside into the crisp darkness. He had prepared for her anger, but this cold, distant expression on her face was so much worse. Amara's temper flared easily, but she was always willing to listen. Though they fought often, Sam always knew she was fighting for them.

"Am—," he started. But that's as far as he got. Amara said nothing in return. So, Sam said nothing too. He wanted to tell her he was sorry, but then he'd be the one in the wrong. He wanted to tell her how scared and tired he was, but then she'd see him as a weakling rather than the strong, confident person she married.

Amara took a step closer. Relief washed over Sam, and he closed his eyes. But then he felt her soft fur brush past his shoulder as she walked back into the house.

Chapter 4

• • • • • • •

Mr. Walnuts

Sam stood outside the house and listened to the cold night wind tear through the trees. Their leaves rustled as loudly as a room full of whispers. Their branches creaked. Their trunks moaned. This forest that had always felt eternal to Sam suddenly seemed so vulnerable. Could these giant oaks and pines and cedars that took so many patient decades to grow strong and tall really vanish in just a matter of months? The wind rippled through Sam's gray fur, and he shivered. Could it be he too was also (just a little) weaker than he'd thought?

Then the sweet sound of Amara's lullaby drifted into the night, and Sam faced the doorway. He didn't know what to say or do, but at the very least he could be home with them. He was about to crawl into the nest when a rock the size of his head crashed into his side.

"Oof!" said Sam—or rather, said the gust of air escaping Sam's mouth.

"Is that you up there, Samuel?" came a gruff voice from somewhere far below. But Sam didn't need to look to know this very particular voice belonged to none other than his boss and the chief nut officer of Nuts for You, Mr. Jack Walnuts. Sam briefly flirted with the idea of holding his breath and staying still, but then another huge rock came flying at his head.

"Sir!" said Sam, "I'm here."

"Well, I don't need you *there*," barked the voice from below, "I need you *here*!"

Sam balled up his fingers into fists and exhaled the rest of the breath he had been holding. This was no time to hide or appear tentative. It was time to be decisive, confident, strong. He raised up his gray tail until it stood straight and proud behind him, and he jumped down to the ground. He landed right beside Jack Walnuts, who was aiming yet another massive rock up at Sam's house.

Mr. Walnuts was a short, stocky copper squirrel, with a giant, bushy tail that flared up all around him like a fire. The angrier he got, the more his tail seemed to rise up and fan out on all sides. Sam did his best not to look at it.

"Mr. Walnuts, sir," said Sam, "I'm here."

"That's clear to me, son," said Mr. Walnuts who still looked like he might throw that rock at Sam. "What is not at all clear to me, is why you are here at home singing lullabies instead of at the office, coming up with a strategy in response to all this condo chatter."

"I wasn't singing lullabies," said Sam.

"I don't give a flying fig what you were singing!" Mr. Walnuts shouted and smashed the rock on the ground. His wild copper tail fanned out farther.

"Yes, sir. I mean no, sir. What I meant was that I was working. I like to bring my work home with me when it's important. That is, every day."

"I see," said Mr. Walnuts, and he narrowed his eyes like he was actually trying to see *through* Sam. "I'm glad you haven't fallen for that work-life balance crap. It's all just a scheme to squeeze more pay for less work out of decent companies."

"Yes, sir," said Sam. "I've been doing a situation assessment, SWOT analysis, and scenario planning ever since I got the news." He paused to gauge his boss's reaction. Had the list of strategic terminology he just spat out sufficiently impressed him? It was hard to tell in the dark.

"Well?"

"Well . . . uh . . ." Sam said, desperately trying to remember an impressive term for having no clue what to do, "it's a volatile situation with a short planning horizon, so I'm doing a continuous environment scan in alignment with our risk appetite to—"

"Okay, okay," Mr. Walnuts interrupted, "you don't have to spell it all out for me. I see you've got it all figured out. Just don't forget the most important thing."

"The most important thing, sir?"

"Know the way—"

"And make them go your way!" Sam shouted like a pup in kindergarten who just figured out that he had the right answer.

"You've got it," Mr. Walnuts chuckled and patted Sam's shoulder with his small, heavy paw. "Now, I want to see this condo rumor squashed and Total Nuts Gathered up by another 10 percent this quarter. Is that understood, son?"

"Yes, sir," said Sam.

"I know it doesn't seem like it now," Mr. Walnuts said with more warmth in his deep voice, "but you're going to be happy this whole thing happened."

"I am?" said Sam.

"You bet your aspen, Samuel. It's situations like these that separate the real leaders from the phonies."

"Yes, sir," said Sam, trying with all his might not to sound like a phony.

CHECK-IN QUESTIONS:
YOUR PRESSURES

Can you relate to Sam's struggle to find the ever-illusive balance between personal and professional commitments? Is there a Mr. Walnuts (or two) in your life? Jot down the pressures weighing you down.

Chapter 5

• • • • • • •

Know the Way

As Sam made his way to the office the next day, he reminded himself that this was his opportunity to prove he was, without a doubt, a great leader. This situation could make his promotion to chief nut officer possible. He repeated it again and again, but deep down, he couldn't help feeling like the chief nothing officer: leader of a doomed business in a vanishing forest.

Sam's only real comfort now was his sturdy business philosophy: Know the way, and make them go your way. It didn't just represent Jack Walnuts but also every strong, confident leader he'd known and the leader he aspired to be. Now he just had to bring these principles to life. And that's exactly what he did when he saw his management team gathered outside his office.

"Here's the plan," Sam said in lieu of a greeting. "We have to gather acorns faster than the forest shrinks. If we work fast enough, we'll have so many nuts it won't matter how many of our trees they chop down and how much of our land they pave over!"

"Great," said Francesca, the finance manager, "except . . . won't it just delay the inevitable? We'll have more market share but in a rapidly shrinking market."

"I've thought of that," said Sam (even though he hadn't). "Once we achieve market dominance, we can steadily increase our prices so we can keep our profit margins high."

"Should we tell our customers what's happening?" asked Mila, the marketing manager.

"No," Sam said so decisively he even impressed himself. "If they find out, they'll panic. And we'll tip off our competitors. The quicker and quieter we work, the better."

"Should we tell the staff?" asked Ravi, the squirrel resources manager.

"No," said Sam even more emphatically. "We can't afford to have them panic either. The less they know, the better."

Francesca started saying something, but Sam cut her off: "And another thing," he said, recalling his late-night talk with Mr. Walnuts, "I think it's time for some stretch goals. Let's adjust our Total Nuts Gathered quota: no raises or bonuses until TNG is 10 percent higher than last quarter."

At this, all three members of his management team gasped, but no one said a word. In fact, no one said anything to Sam at all until his all-paws announcement to the branch later that day. Jack Walnuts held company town-hall meetings twice a year to give updates and the occasional burst of inspiration. He always looked so leader-like standing atop a tree stump before his rapt audience. Sam decided this was the perfect time for him to step up and present the inspiring new gathering target as part of his (literal) stump speech to his staff. And so, he did.

At first, there was a kind of silence that could only be described as "stunned," and then somebody coughed and raised a paw.

"Would you please let us know why we are raising the target?" asked a clear, bright voice in the back of the crowd. And Sam felt a shadow of dread pass over him when he realized it was Paloma—a longtime employee everyone at the branch seemed to look up to, even though she had no team and no authority. Sam glanced, then glared at his management team, but they said nothing.

"Why raise the target?" Sam repeated. He thought back to Jack Walnuts and his wildfire tail. Would he stand for this kind of insubordination? Never. Would he blame Sam for his employees' behavior? Absolutely. So, Sam stomped his foot and said, "Because you can all do better. You can all *be* better. If you work hard enough, you can be the best in the whole forest!" Then, seeing only blank stares in response, he added, "And when you gather enough nuts, you get your bonus."

"So," said Paloma, "it's not because a forest recession is coming?" A murmur and then a rumble passed through the crowd. Sam puffed up his chest and exuded as much confidence as he could muster, and a little extra.

"You have nothing to worry about," he said. "I've got it all under control."

But over the next few days, it began to become clear that he, in fact, did not. Instead of productivity going up, it actually declined. And instead of nut sales soaring, they began to slump.

Chapter 6

. . . .

Make Them Go Your Way

"Why are they all so far behind on their quotas?" Sam demanded as soon as Ravi stepped into his office in the morning. Ravi seemed to contemplate stepping back out, then sighed and stayed put.

"And which, uh . . . quotas are you referring to?" he asked.

"All of them," said Sam.

"Right," said Ravi, "I know it looks bad." He ran his paw over the bald patch on his head and kept it there, rubbing what seemed to be a headache. This appeared to be his entire response.

"So, tell me what you're doing about it, Ravi," said Sam.

"Well, squirrel resources tried to lead a training session to increase productivity . . . but the trouble is no one showed up."

"No one showed up?" Sam repeated. "Then fire them!"

"Fire them?"

"Yes, fire them," said Sam, "and get me new squirrels who actually want to work." He didn't like the idea of anyone losing their job, but he liked the idea of losing his job even less. Was he the only one who understood the desperate urgency of this situation?

"Well, um, they've tried," said Ravi. "They're already trying to hire more squirrels, but the candidate pipeline is actually shrinking."

"Shrinking?"

"Getting smaller."

"I know what shrinking means!" Sam shouted, surprised to find himself standing up. He sat back down and, as calmly as he could (which wasn't particularly calm), asked Ravi to call in Francesca and Mila.

"Let's talk sales," said Sam as soon as they walked into his office. Mila clasped her paws together and the tip of her tail trembled.

"I've tried everything I can think of," she said. "I paid for ads, I launched a re-fur-ral campaign, I even ran a flash sale. It's still not enough."

"I'm sorry, but you're just not holding your teams accountable," said Francesca. Mila and Ravi both shot her a betrayed look, but Francesca folded her arms to signal she was perfectly satisfied with her own perspective.

"How can I hold them accountable when they don't even know why we've increased our targets?" Mila pleaded. "Plus, they're already overworked. If I push them any harder, they're just going to quit."

"If I hear any more excuses *I* might quit," Sam snapped. He felt pretty good about this retort but was also dimly aware the expression on their faces looked perhaps more like hope than horror. He thought of Mr. Walnuts and his pronouncement that it's situations like these that separate the real leaders from the phonies. *What would Jack Walnuts do?* "I know," said Sam, and his paws went cold. "Let's just cut their benefits. No more vacation days until we hit our target. We have to stop behaving like these squirrels are doing us a favor by being here. They work for us and not the other way around. So, let's start acting like real leaders and make them go our way."

After completing this pep talk and watching his management team slink out of his office, Sam didn't feel particularly peppy himself. So, he power-posed for a full minute, pulling back his shoulders and sticking out his chin. But his gray tail slumped behind him like a wilting flower. He pulled at the heavy wooden door to his acorn safe, but he quickly realized it was too full to open without the nuts tumbling out. He'd hoped the sight of his branch's reserves would revive his spirits. This great collection was meant to fund the staff's end-of-year shellabration. Now it wasn't even enough to get them through the winter. Sam needed more acorns, and he needed them fast. So, he took a deep breath and decided the best thing to do was what he had always done best: get back to gathering. This was something he could do now and do better than anyone else.

Refreshed by this plan, he strung all the nut satchels he had over his shoulder and flung himself over the edge of his office entrance. He told himself he would return with such a bounty of acorns that his staff would gather around him and beg to hear his words of wisdom. He would no longer just be their boss but also their hero. He would not only save his branch but also their entire forest. Sam carried this comforting thought with him into the thickest, darkest parts of the forest, foraging with more intensity than ever before. The only trouble was that nearly all of the acorns were gone.

CHECK-IN QUESTIONS: YOUR STYLE UNDER STRESS

The condo challenge is not bringing out the best in Sam. Reflect on how your own leadership style changes under stress. How does that change impact you and your team?

Chapter 7

• • • • • • •

Lost in the Darkness

The sky far overhead turned a dusty purple, and a cold, smoky mist wound through the bases of the trees. It was so thick Sam couldn't make out the roots that cradled all the fallen nuts. Dusk settled in quickly, and the night birds began to practice their calls. Sam no longer felt secure about his present, let alone his future. He'd gone so far away from his home base that he didn't recognize any of the trees.

He realized he was hungry, and thirsty too. Even though stopping would be dangerous, trying to outrun a predator on an empty stomach could be even more disastrous. So, Sam darted into the fog and pressed his back against a tree. He shoved one arm into a satchel and rummaged through the meager stash of nuts while keeping his eyes peeled for danger. He bit into the first one he drew out of his bag and winced in pain.

The sound of his own cry startled him so much he dropped all his satchels and clasped his paw over his mouth. His heart thumped so loudly in his ears that, for a moment, he couldn't tell if someone was stomping toward him. Then he thought the bigger danger would be a heart attack. But after several minutes, he calmed down enough to take full breaths and even let them out with minimal shakiness. The acorn he tried to bite into must have been too green: a rookie mistake. The rest of the nuts were swallowed up by the mist and lost to the darkness.

What would Mr. Walnuts think now of his unsuccessful successor? How could his employees see him as their leader, let alone their hero? But he'd done all the leadership things he was supposed to do, hadn't he? He had a clear vision. He pushed his staff to follow the way. He clocked sixteen hours of work every day and slept just eight hours a night (which sounds like a lot but is about half as much time as the average squirrel spends sleeping). It wasn't his fault that his management team was incapable of managing and his workers were unwilling to work. Sam was about to wallow in another self-pitying thought, but just then, he felt a grasp on his shoulder.

"Ah!" shrieked Sam. He spun around to face his attacker, then shrieked again when he saw a gray squirrel, just like him, standing behind him with an amused expression on her face. Sam's paws flew up into fists. The squirrel's eyes opened in surprise, and she burst out laughing.

"I'm sorry," she gasped, clutching her white belly. "I must have scared your tail off."

"Who, me?" said Sam and slowly lowered his paws. "I wasn't scared."

"No?"

"No! I was ready to protect my turf."

At this, the gray squirrel laugh-cried some more. Then she noticed Sam wasn't laughing and wiped her bright, black eyes.

"Oh, no. Now I'm sorry again. I thought you were kidding about your turf. I saw you crouching beside the tree and assumed you were lost."

"I wasn't crouching," said Sam. "I was . . . lounging."

"Okay," said the squirrel. "My mistake. Have a good night!"

"Wait," said Sam. "I wasn't crouching, but I was lost—*am* lost. This is not my neck of the woods. And, well, I need a safe place to sleep. I'll be on my way home first thing in the morning. I run a very important business, and things will fall apart if I don't get back quickly." The small gray squirrel studied Sam more soberly this time.

"I can show you a nest no one has used in months up in a tree right there," she said, "or," her eyes twinkled, "I can show you my community. What do you think?"

"Yeah, thanks," said Sam, "I'm sure your community is great. But as I said, my employees need me back immediately, if not sooner."

"*Oaky*-dokey," shrugged the squirrel. "The tree is right this way. Would you like to go now, or would you like to stop for a snack?" Just the sound of the word *snack* made Sam's stomach growl. The squirrel giggled. "I'll take that as a yes!" She slipped her satchel off her slim shoulder and tossed him the whole bundle. He shoved his arm inside and froze. He was elbow-deep in perfectly plump, smooth acorns.

"Where did you get these?" he whispered, as though the sound of his voice would spook away this tiny treasure in his arms.

"We have plenty in our community," said the squirrel. "Is there a shortage in your parts?"

"Not a shortage exactly," said Sam slowly, still clutching the wonderful little parcel.

"No?"

"No. Just a short-term constraint in our supply chain."

"Ah, that does sound different."

"So, this community of yours has lots of acorns for sale?" Sam pressed.

"Oh, we have so many acorns now we don't even sell them anymore. You could say we have the whole market *acornered*."

"Don't sell them?" Sam shouted, so disturbed by this idea that he totally missed her pun. He hugged the satchel to his chest and was about to release a fully loaded lecture on the importance of market dominance when he noticed the bemused look on her face and stopped. Why reveal his hard-earned business secrets to someone who was too naive to recognize the extent of her own advantage? He clearly had the upper paw here, and he had better keep it that way.

"Shall I show you to that nest now?" asked the squirrel.

"No," said Sam, "I'd like to see your community."

You've now reached the part of the journey where everything is about to change. Sam will leave his familiar world and never see it the same way again. He will discover new ways of working, learning, and living that only become possible when you understand the nature of power. He'll come to know what power is, how it works, why it matters, and what it means to lead together. But before you venture forward with him, take a moment to look back.

CHECK-IN QUESTIONS

- *What have you noticed so far about Sam's approach to using power? What are the consequences of his leadership philosophy for him and those around him?*

- *What do you think power is? How would you define it?*

- *Now comes the fun part: consider yourself. After all, that's why we're all really here, isn't it? How do you use your own power (or choose not to)? What positive and negative impacts do these choices have on you and on others?*

Each of us uses our power and reacts to power every day, but we rarely notice it. Once you know what to look for, you can't unsee it. And once you can see power in action, you can change it.

Ready to see your own world in a new way?

PART II

THE POWER-WITH COMMUNITY

Chapter 8

• • • • • • •

Mary Parker Forest

The two squirrels trudged together through the cold, dark, smokey forest. Sam clutched the bundle of acorns to his chest, while the small gray squirrel skipped ahead. He kept his eyes fixed on the bright white tip of her question-mark-shaped tail and did his best to keep up.

"Looks like you do this a lot," he said, trying to mask that he was out of breath.

"Our community is often on the move," said the squirrel. "How about yours?"

"Our forest hasn't changed in generations," Sam said proudly.

"I'm sorry to hear that," said the squirrel.

Sam hurried to correct her, but she bounded away before he could speak. All he could do was follow this strange squirrel in silence, watching her white-tipped tail dart through the darkness like a firefly in the night.

By the time they reached a clearing and the ground turned soft and warm underfoot, Sam was too tired to take in his surroundings. The squirrel showed him to a roomy, dry hollow in a log, lined with plenty of fresh oak leaves for cushion. Sam was too exhausted to eat, so he curled up inside the log with the satchel. He was about to let the sleep rush in, but his eyes popped open.

"Wait," he said to the squirrel. "What's your name?"

"I'm Mary Parker Forest," said the gray squirrel.

"I'm Sam Squirrel," said Sam, and he closed his eyes.

What seemed like seconds later, sunshine beamed into his alcove in the log. Sam stretched with a satisfying squeak at the end and threw his arm over his sleeping wife. But, of course, it wasn't his wife. He was spooning a bag of acorns. He sat up and bumped his head on the ceiling. Amara! Would she be worried he didn't come home last night or just annoyed, thinking he'd pulled another all-nighter at the office? What had she told Josie and Remi? And what would his management team members think of his disappearance? Would they report it to Mr. Walnuts? Worst of all, would everyone's productivity plummet?

He grabbed the satchel and tumbled out of the log, noticing too late that it was higher than he remembered. He landed right on his face, but it didn't hurt. A soft, green moss carpeted the forest. Two small gray feet stood beside his head. Sam looked up to find Mary once again bent over in laughter, her question-mark tail bouncing behind her.

"Good morning," she said. "Nice of you to *drop* by."

"Funny," said Sam. He brushed himself off and slung the satchel over his shoulder. "It was kind of you to lend me a paw last night. I just need one more favor. Take me to your leader."

"You sound like an alien," said Mary. "What kind of a leader would you like to meet?"

"Not *a* leader," said Sam, his patience evaporating with the morning dew, "*the* leader. The person in charge."

"In charge of what?"

"In charge of this place."

"I see," said Mary, "but that's not possible because—"

"Look, I get that you can't just have strangers marching in and demanding an appointment," Sam cut in, "but I'll make sure you're rewarded. Believe me."

"I do believe you, Sam," said Mary, her voice growing calmer as Sam's grew sharper. "It's just that we don't have just one squirrel in charge. There's way too much we want to accomplish, and things move too quickly around here for that. We have many leaders, and we lead together. How about you tell me what's behind your request so I can try to find the right person?"

Sam narrowed his eyes. She was clever, this one. She clearly wanted him to expose his weakness so she could use it to her advantage. But he decided to play her game: "There's a condo development going up in our forest in a few months," he said. "Pretty soon, we won't have enough food to go around. You have plenty of acorns. But there must be something you don't have. I'd like to propose a trade."

"I see," said Mary, her face finally growing serious. "I'm not sure how we can help, but how about I show you around? Maybe we'll find something to trade. Or maybe you'll bring home some ideas that will feed your community even better than our acorns could."

Sam scoffed at the suggestion. What could he possibly learn from this odd squirrel and her silly community that gives all its nuts away for free? Then again, what if this was his way in to find the community's leader? It's not as though he'd be keeping his wife and kids waiting. By now, Amara would be off to work and the pups at elemen-tree school. His staff would just have to muddle through without him a little while longer.

"Okay," said Sam at last.

"Then off we go!" sang out Mary.

She scampered up a large, craggy stone, then another and another, until she reached a tall boulder. Sam climbed after her, higher and higher. The sky overhead was a vibrant blue, and white clouds floated by at a leisurely pace. Could it be that they were shaped like acorns? No, Sam, realized, it was just his hunger catching up to him. He reached for his bag of acorns, but a gust of wind shoved him, and the satchel slipped off his shoulder. He stretched out his arm to grasp it, but another blast of wind sent it tumbling over the edge.

He glanced back up and felt his paws grow cold when he saw no one ahead. The wind whistled in Sam's ears and rustled his fur. He had just started to wonder whether this was some kind of elaborate trap when Mary's sharp little face poked out over the edge of the stone.

"Here we are!" she shouted.

Sam pulled himself up to the top of the big rock and gasped at what he saw.

Chapter 9

A Whole New Squorld

"Welcome to our *squorld*!" said Mary, and chuckled (alone) at her joke. Sam stared down from the massive rock, speechless. Beneath that sharp blue sky, sunlight beamed down onto a juicy green prairie encircled by towering, ancient trees. Birds seemed to turn into streaks of color, and the air rang with their cheerful calls. Purple dragonflies dove straight down and darted back up, just for the joy of it. Mary grabbed a vine on the side of the rock and leapt down, her question-mark tail unfurling like a cape behind her. Sam jumped down after her and tried to take in all his surroundings as the ground rushed up to meet him.

He was surprised to see this strange colony wasn't just made up of tree squirrels and flying squirrels but also every kind of squirrel Sam could imagine—and even some he never had. There were gray, black, red, brown, copper, orange, white, calico, and even a few giant purple squirrels, with tails nearly two feet long. Some squirrels were happily relaxing or working alone. Some bunched together in animated clusters.

Sam landed with a soft thump and looked around in amazement. A sweet mix of autumn leaves, turned earth, and wild apples filled his nose. Bunches of fat acorns glistened in the sunshine all around them. What was this place so close to but so different from his own home? The squirrels in his part of the forest stuck to their own kind. Their postures were always tense. Their movements always frantic. If the squirrels back home spotted an acorn on the ground, they would have already snatched it up.

He winced at the thought of home. This was all so terribly, so completely unfair. Spurred by an irresistible wave of envy, Sam dashed over to a sprawling oak tree, grabbed an acorn, and shoved it into his cheek. His mouth watered as that sweet nutty flavor spread across his tongue, in sharp contrast to the bitterness he felt inside.

"Well, hello there!" called an unfamiliar voice behind him.

Sam spun around, his fists raised, his tail like a gray spike behind him. He gulped down the half-chewed acorn and tried to look as ferocious as he could manage.

"Goodness, this is one ferocious squirrel," said the voice.

Sam saw no one and spun around again, ready for battle. Mary smiled and pointed down. Sam hopped back. At his feet stood a black chipmunk with wisps of gray in his fur. He was about half Sam's height but stood upright with the confidence of a much bigger creature.

"Sam Squirrel, I am delighted to introduce you to our professor, Alfie Akorn," said Mary.

"Hello, Professor Akorn!" said Sam, as he executed an awkward combination of a bow and wave. (Cross-cultural communication was never his strong suit.)

"Call me Alfie," said Alfie. "We're not big on status symbols here. There is a lot we want to accomplish, and status symbols just tend to slow things down, don't you think?"

"Yes, sir. I mean, Alfie . . . sir," said Sam. "You must be in charge here."

"I certainly am." A bright grin lit up the professor's bushy little face, and Sam felt a gust of relief, mixed with nervous excitement. It surged through him for one glorious moment, then crashed down just as suddenly when Alfie added, "Though, most of us are in charge of something here."

"Right," Sam muttered.

"Alfie is a brilliant educator," said Mary, "and these days, he leads our university. If you want to learn what we think helps our community flourish, he's the perfect teacher. That is, if you're willing to do a bit of early morning teaching, Alfie?"

"I always want to teach when someone wants to learn," said Alfie, with a quick flash of his chipmunk teeth. What Sam actually wanted was to tell them both to go take a long walk off a short branch. But more than that, he wanted their acorns. If he had to sit through a boring lecture to get what he wanted, then so be it.

"Willing and eager," said Sam. Mary hopped up and clapped as though he'd just given her a present. Alfie looked Sam up and down and awarded him with a small, approving nod.

"Then let's get started," he said. And to Sam's surprise, the two strange creatures turned and began to walk off.

Chapter 10

• • • • • • •

The Tour Begins

"Wait," called Sam. "I thought you were going to tell me about this place!"

"Oh, I can tell you all about what I think of our community," said Alfie, "but what really matters is what *you* think. And for you to think anything at all, you'll need to come to your own conclusions. What do you say?"

Sam said nothing for fear of stretching out the lesson any longer than it needed to be. To keep himself from talking, he tossed another plump acorn into his mouth and concentrated on it as they walked. But Alfie surprised him with another question.

"Exshcoosh ma?" Sam mumbled through his very full mouth.

"What do you notice?" Alfie repeated, his small dark eyes set on Sam's face.

"Um . . ." Sam said, trying to guess the right answer. He hadn't noticed much of anything aside from the juicy acorn in his mouth and his intense dedication to getting through this lesson with minimal effort and maximum speed. But now Sam looked around and saw they'd strolled into the lush green prairie he saw on his trip down the big rock. Small groups of squirrels congregated in animated conversation.

"Well . . ." said Sam, his curiosity emerging despite his best efforts to stay disengaged, "there are many different kinds of squirrels here. And I'm not sure what it is they all care about, but they seem to care about it a whole lot."

"How can you tell?" asked Alfie.

"They all seem to have something to say," said Sam, taking in all those excited voices and lively gestures, "and it looks like they're really listening."

"Anything else?"

"Actually, yes," said Sam. "I can't figure out who's in charge."

"That's Sam's favorite question," Mary teased, but Alfie nodded solemnly.

"And what's important to you about that, Sam?" he asked.

"I don't know," Sam admitted, startled a bit by the sound of those words coming out of his own mouth. "What are they doing, anyway?" he asked, in an unsubtle attempt to change the subject.

"This is our university," said Mary. "We've been gathering here every morning to share what we know ever since we realized how much power there is in learning from each other."

Just then, a blonde, wavy-furred marmot sitting in a circle of squirrels looked up at them and waved. This was his chance, Sam thought. He puffed up his chest and tail to show he was important somewhere, even if not specifically here.

"Hi there," he said to the group, "would you please tell me who's in charge here?"

"In charge of what?" asked the marmot, and that's when Sam lost all of his remaining cool.

"In charge of this place!" he snapped. "In charge of all your resources. In charge of making all the decisions. I don't understand why you're all keeping it a big secret!"

The group fell silent. The marmot cracked her knuckles and slowly brought herself up to a standing position until she towered over Sam. With his head now at the level of the tall marmot's hip, Sam's outrage swiftly cooled. He was a tall squirrel, as far as gray squirrels went. Not since he was a pup had he stood beside someone who made him feel so small. The marmot looked down at Sam, and then, to his immense relief, she smiled.

"I'm happy to tell you," she said. "We don't keep secrets around here. Our community has a lot to get done, and secrets just slow things down and cause more problems than they solve."

"Uh, well, thanks," said Sam, backing away a bit, just to be on the safe side. "I appreciate it. I'm Sam Squirrel, by the way."

"I'm Tiziana Cashewrow," said Tiziana Cashewrow, and she gave him another warm smile from high above. Then she nodded at Alfie. "And this tiny yet mighty professor you see here leads our university," she said. "That means he's in charge of helping us achieve the university's purpose. And each of the squirrels you see on campus today is responsible for teaching what they've learned over the past week so we can all grow stronger as a community."

"You're trying to tell me you've all got something to teach?" Sam sneered. Did these squirrels have no respect for higher education? Back home there was just one prestigious university that proudly rejected most squirrels who applied. The lectures were led by a handful of scholars. And it took them most of their lives to earn their degrees and achieve their status.

"Of course," said the marmot.

"In this group, we're teaching each other about predator deception," chimed in a shiny brown chipmunk in the group. "I'm Julie Bats, by the way," she said with a wave, "and this here is Erich Furmm. He just showed our group how to make rattlesnake perfume!" The whole group cheered. And the spotted ground squirrel who must have been Erich smiled bashfully and waved off the chipmunk.

"Oh, stop it, Julie," he said shyly. "It's the least I could do."

"Those squirrels over by the maple tree are studying advanced nest-building," said Tiziana, the marmot. "Back there is a group doing language practice. And over to the left, the prairie dogs are teaching everyone tunneling skills."

"Prairie dogs are squirrels?" Sam asked in a whisper.

"Yep, and so are marmots," said the marmot. "But don't worry. I had no idea."

"See?" shouted Julie, the chipmunk. "You're learning already!" And the whole group burst into hearty laughter.

"We've all learned a lot since we formed this community," said Mary, who by now, must have figured out Sam wasn't a fan of being laughed at. "And there's one thing we're learning about together that's more important than all the rest."

"Okay," said Sam. "I'll bite. What's the most important thing you're learning about?"

CHECK-IN QUESTIONS:
YOUR WORKPLACE

* *How does your workplace compare to Mary's community so far?*

* *In what ways is your team or workplace diverse? In what ways is it homogenous?*

* *Do all members of your group contribute equally to conversations? Why or why not?*

* *Is it obvious who holds the most power? How could you tell from a distance?*

Chapter 11

· · · · · · ·

Defining Power

"We're learning about power," said Mary.

"Power?" Sam repeated. "You mean like having control over others?"

"Well, a power-over approach is one common way to use power," said Julie, the chipmunk, "and it's true that most of us assume power is dirty or cruel. But it doesn't have to be that way."

"Right," said Tiziana. "Having control over others is just one way you can *use* power. It's not what power *is*."

"Okay," said Sam, glancing at the acorns scattered about the prairie. "Then power is having something others need."

"You're getting warmer," said Tiziana. "You can *gain* power when you control access to something rare and valuable, particularly resources that create a sense of safety or self-esteem. And you can also gain power by having the ability to take access to something valuable *away*."

"Like employee benefits," said Sam, and he felt his face flush.

"That's right," said Alfie.

"Or attention," said Sam, thinking now of how small and powerless he felt at home ever since Amara began to look through him as though he didn't exist.

"That's right," said Alfie. "So, you can *gain* power by granting access to something valuable or by taking access away. But what do you think power *is*, Sam?" he asked.

Sam paused to think about it. He had wanted to have more power almost as far back as he could remember. But had he ever stopped to consider what power really was? And what did having more power get him, anyway? He felt his shoulders straighten and his chest rise as he thought back to his first promotion to a manager role at Nuts for You, Inc.

"Go get 'em, son," Jack Walnuts had said in his gravelly voice with a pat on Sam's shoulder. In that moment, Sam felt as if he could accomplish anything. As if Mr. Walnuts had strapped a tiny rocket to his back that could carry him all the way to his wildest dreams.

Sam thought of the chilly morning his twins were born and how proud he felt that he could protect them from the cold with the strong walls of his pine house. Together, he and Amara looked out at the fog that lay atop the horizon like cold, white foam and felt they had the power to give their pups a childhood better than anything they ever had.

Then Sam thought of the acorn-stuffed safe in his office and wondered why it had always made him feel so good. It must be because all those shiny nuts reminded him that his branch had power. That meant Sam could do anything he wanted: protect himself and his family from harm, command more respect, and make just about anyone go his way.

"I think I've got it figured out," Sam said. "Power is the capacity to get things done."[2]

"Well said," said Tiziana, who still stood towering over Sam. "And when you have more power, you have fewer limits on what you can do."

"I guess I never thought about it that way," said Sam.

"Do you see now why it's so important for us to learn about power?" Mary asked with something like a quiet reverence in her voice.

"I think so," said Sam. "Because if power is the capacity to get things done and you want to achieve something, you're going to need some power."

"Exactly!" cried Erich, the ground squirrel, then clasped his paw over his mouth. The chipmunk beside him softly patted his back, and he let his paw drop. "Thanks, Julie," he said. Then he turned to Sam: "I'm pretty new here, so I'm still getting used to having the power to speak up. All this freedom is wonderful, but it can be scary too."

"Scary?" said Sam. "How can freedom be scary?"

"Well," said Erich thoughtfully, "I guess when someone has power over us, it can create a sense of security. Sort of like the comfort of parents or experts doing our thinking for us. We might resent their authority and crave the freedom to run our own lives, but once we get that freedom, it can be overwhelming at first. Honestly, I'm so used to following orders that now I worry I'll make the wrong decision or say the wrong thing."

"I get it," said Julie. "It takes time to get used to having power and to trust it's safe to use. And thank you for choosing to speak up more. Your ideas have already made us stronger."

Sam studied this bizarre exchange in a cloud of bewilderment. Here were squirrels who had almost infinite acorns along with prized skills and knowledge. They understood power meant the capacity to get things done and seemed to have big plans for their community. But instead of growing their power by keeping their valuable resources scarce, they scattered all that precious power like empty nut shells. They even went out of their way to encourage each other to use the power they already had. And yet, Sam had to admit they seemed happier and healthier than any squirrels he'd ever met.

"Okay, I'll be honest," said Sam (with actual honesty). "I'm impressed by what I've seen so far, but I can't make heads or tails of it. If you've learned so much about power, why doesn't anyone around here seem to care about growing it?"

"Oh, but we do!" said Mary. "It's what we care about most of all."

"Then why is it that all you seem to care about is giving your power away?" Sam insisted.

"Because you're right," said Alfie. "We care very much about giving power away." Sam felt that confusing blend of frustration and wonder gnaw away at him from the inside.

"Then why," he said carefully, trying not to let his voice betray his agitation, "don't you have more squirrels trying to keep as much power as they can for themselves?"

"Because that would just hold back the collective power of our community," said Mary, "which would put a big damper on personal power too."

Sam let out a small, exasperated sigh. He was starting to feel like he might be stuck in a dream where everything made just enough sense to be realistic but not enough sense to be real.

"Maybe this would all become clearer if you visited our laboratory," suggested Erich with slightly more confidence.

"That's a great idea," said Julie, the chipmunk. "Besides," she added with a wink at Tiziana, "Dasher is always looking for more squirrels to experiment on."

CHECK-IN QUESTIONS:
PERSPECTIVES ON POWER

Take a moment now to consider your own views on power.

- *Do you have negative or positive associations with power that you'd like to update?*

- *Where would you like to have more power, and why?*

- *Where does the weight of your power (e.g., autonomy, authority, responsibility) feel too heavy or overwhelming? What might make it easier for you to use your power?*

Chapter 12

. . . .

Too Little Power

Sam said goodbye to the peculiar group of professors and students at the university and followed Mary and Alfie up a steep, grassy hill. By the time he caught up to them, they were already chatting with someone at the mouth of a giant log. It was a slim, blond prairie dog who stood upright, holding a platter of fresh bark topped with dewy wildflowers.

"Sam Squirrel, please meet Dasher Keltner," said Alfie.

"And before you ask, he's the scientist in charge of this logratory," said Mary.

"It's nice to meet you, Dr. Keltner," said Sam.

"Call me Dasher," said the prairie dog.

"Because status symbols just slow things down?" asked Sam, even though he wasn't quite sure he understood what Alfie had meant by it earlier.

"Sure," said Dasher with a smile, "and because I quite like my first name."

"It suits you," said Alfie. "You get a whole lot done around here pretty fast."

Mary laughed, and Dasher extended the platter of colorful wild-flowers to the group. They each popped a flower in their mouths. The delicate sweetness of it quickly melted across Sam's tongue. He had never tasted anything quite like it.

"Do you all consent to taking part in our experiments?" said Dasher with mock gravity.

"I do," said Alfie.

"For sure," said Mary.

"Sign me up," said Sam, feeling refreshed by the succulent snack.

"Then step right in!"

Sam hopped up to the opening of the laboratory and entered the cool, darkened cave of the hollow log. Inside, squirrels dashed back and forth between rooms carved into the branches.

"Dasher and his scientist friends here study the psychology of power," said Mary. "They're learning all sorts of things that help us use power more thoughtfully in our community."

"Interesting," said Sam (because he was actually starting to feel interested). "And what have you discovered so far?"

"Take a look," said Dasher, and he walked the group over to one of the small rooms, motioning to them to be quiet.

Inside, Sam saw a red squirrel seated on a pile of leaves, squinting at a fierce ray of sunshine streaming in through a hole in the log. The squirrel tried to turn away, but the hot light still pierced his eyes. He squirmed for a while, then covered his face and sat motionless.

"This is an experiment my colleagues are conducting,"[3] Dasher whispered. "They've asked this participant to wait here until they get back, and they carved that hole in the wall so the light streams in and makes it a pretty uncomfortable experience.

"Before they asked him to wait, they instructed him to think of a time he felt powerless. He told them the story of a micromanager he used to have. She would tell him what to do, how to do it, and when to do it, and then she stood over him making sure he did everything exactly as she wanted."

Sam looked again at the lone squirrel, hunched in a small ball in the middle of the room. Then Dasher motioned to the room next door. Sam peered in and saw another squirrel in an identical room pierced by a harsh sunbeam. This squirrel blinked into the sun a few times, then stood up, marched over to the hole, and plugged it up with a clump of leaves on the ground.

"Now that's one smart squirrel," said Sam, instantly relating to the more confident creature.

"I'm not sure these squirrels are so different," said Dasher. "In fact, they both had the same overbearing manager. But this squirrel was asked to think about a time when he felt powerful. He drew himself up and described the day he and his coworker both quit that job with the micromanager. And it's not just these two squirrels either. We've found when someone feels powerless, they avoid taking risks, and they tend to think more conventionally. But when they feel powerful—"

"They take action," Sam said as he glanced back at the hunched squirrel covering his face.

"That's right," said Dasher. "They feel more confident and optimistic. They share their opinions even if others disagree. And they think more creatively." [4]

"I guess they also feel happier," said Sam, thinking wistfully of a time not long ago when he had felt unstoppable as the company's newest and most promising branch leader.

"Exactly," said Dasher. "Feeling powerful increases our well-being. It gives us the freedom to feel and act like our real selves. On the other paw, feeling powerless causes stress, anxiety, and even a shortened lifespan."[5]

Sam looked at Mary and Alfie with a hint of respect for the first time since he'd met them. Perhaps they were on to something after all.

"I think I get it now," he said. "You want the squirrels in your community to feel powerful so they can be proactive and resourceful, so they can get things done."

"We want them to feel powerful and *be* powerful," said Mary.

"But not too powerful," Dasher added.

"Why not?" Sam exclaimed. "Isn't it better to have more power?"

"Yes," said Alfie. "When you have more *collective* power, you can achieve more."

"See?" said Sam smugly to Dasher.

"And also no," said Alfie. "It's not always better for the individual or the community if someone keeps amassing more *personal* power."

Sam huffed. He grabbed the last wildflower off Dasher's plate and shoved it in his mouth. He chomped it loudly as small, wet petal bits flew from his mouth. Why were these strange squirrels always talking in riddles? Why was he wasting his precious time here instead of traveling home to reassure his family and motivate his employees? Why couldn't he be more like the humans and just take their acorns by force? He was so distracted by his frustrated musings that it took him awhile to notice Mary, Alfie, and Dasher all watching his face with giddy amusement.

Chapter 13

• • • • • • •

Too Much Power

"Debrief him! Debrief him!" Mary shouted, hopping up and down.

"You want him to do what to me?"

"Sam," said Dasher with a sparkling smile, "thank you for participating in our pilot experiment.[6] Would you like to hear how it works?" Sam narrowed his eyes and nodded, so the scientist continued. "We offer our participants delicious wildflowers while they're engaged in an activity. And we place just enough flowers on the plate so there's one for each person and one left over. We run this experiment with high-power and low-power participants. Do you want to guess what results we tend to see?"

Sam glanced at the now-empty plate with a sudden wave of embarrassment. Had he really eaten the last flower without asking if anyone else wanted it? His mother would not approve. But the evidence was right there on the empty plate and in his formerly full mouth.

"I guess participants who feel powerful take the last flower," he said without making eye contact with anyone in the group.

"That's right!" Dasher practically sang out. "And even more fascinating, they also tend to chew with their mouths open and get crumbs all over themselves and the floor."

Sam quickly wiped his face and brushed away the stray bits of chewed up petals on the ground. Even his pups would have had better manners.

"So, are you saying squirrels who take what they want go on to become more powerful?" he asked in search of a comforting explanation.

"Actually, no," said Dasher. "More often than not, it works the other way around."

"The other way around?"

"Yep. We tend to think greedy or corrupt individuals get all the power. But our data reveals the opposite. It's the collaborative, empathetic folks who tend to earn power most easily."

"Yeah, okay," said Sam. "Maybe that's true in touchy-feely industries, but I cannot believe it's true in places where you need to be tough to get things done."

"You cannot or you *walnut*?" said Mary, and everyone rolled their eyes.

"We thought so too at first," said Dasher, "but our research shows it holds up across many industries.[7] For example, we've found that politicians and hedge fund managers who show more empathy and care for others earn more trust and achieve better results. Only something strange starts to happen to most individuals when they amass *too much* personal power."

"They eat with their mouths open?" Sam sneered.

"Yep," said Dasher. "But it's the reason they eat with their mouths open that's so interesting. Our research shows that when we have too much power, we lose our inhibitions and become self-centered.[8] Power can reduce our perspective-taking, impulse-control, and—"

"Number of wildflowers!" Sam cut in.

"How helpful," said Alfie. "Sam has just demonstrated another fascinating research finding. Having too much power makes us more likely to interrupt others and to overtalk."[9]

"Uhh . . . you're welcome?" Sam said, and Mary sent him a playful wink.

"And it gets worse," said Dasher. "When we have too much power, we're more likely to take dangerous risks[10] and make snap judgments.[11] We're also more likely to break rules and even be abusive toward others, all without taking personal responsibility for our actions."[12]

"Hang on now," said Sam. "You're just describing a few bad apples."

"I'm afraid not," said Dasher. "It's not that all squirrels who have power are fundamentally bad. It's that getting hopped up on too much power makes many of us behave badly, which hurts those around us and eventually ourselves too."

"Can't you just teach leaders empathy skills, then?" Sam asked, vaguely recalling it as a topic at some leadership conference he had to attend.

"Trying to teach someone with too much power how to feel empathy is a little like trying to teach someone who's too full how to feel hungry," said Mary.

"Exactly," said Alfie. "Most of us feel empathy naturally when power is distributed well. So, the problem isn't so much a scarcity of skill as it is a glut of power."[13]

"It's almost as though having too much power becomes a kind of brain injury,"[14] said Dasher. "It clouds over the parts of our brains that let us interact well with others."

"Brain injury?" Sam cried. "If that's true, then why are you all going around trying to make everyone here more powerful?"

"Our goal is to find a good balance of power," said Mary. "Think of distributing power like keeping a plant healthy. Give the plant too little water, and it will starve. Give it too much water, and it will drown."

Sam pressed his paw to his forehead to keep his head from spinning. This was all much too much for him to make sense of. He marched back to the doorway of the lab for a breath of fresh air. But just as he reached the opening, he crashed into a tall squirrel with stark white fur.

CHECK-IN QUESTIONS: POWER AT PLAY

Reflect on your own observations of power:

- *Think of a person or group that has felt powerless. How has it impacted those people or the people around them ?*

- *Think of a person or group with too much power. How has it impacted those people or the people around them?*

- *How about you? On a scale of 1 to 10, how satisfied are you with how much power you have at work? How about in other areas of life?*

Chapter 14

• • • • • • •

Formal and Informal Power

"Peater!" Mary cried. "I hoped we'd run into you, but not so literally."

"Mary," said the tall squirrel in a deep, warm voice, "you always keep me on my toes."

"Meet our social psychologist, Peater Tree Coleman," said Mary. "Peater, meet Sam Squirrel. He's been learning about power so he could bring more of it to his business."

"That's right," Sam spoke up (just in case this Peater person was somebody worth impressing). "I think I have it pretty much figured out now."

"We were just talking about personal and collective power," said Alfie.

"Wonderful," said Peater. "Have you discussed the other two types of power we study?"[15]

"Not yet," said Dasher.

"What are they?" asked Sam, though he already felt pretty sure he had both of them.

"Well, if you think of the employees at your company with the greatest ability to get things done, what would you say gives them that power?" asked Peater.

Sam instantly thought of himself, but, in a show of humility (because he deduced by now they liked that sort of thing), he changed course: "There's my boss, Jack Walnuts," said Sam. "He's our chief nut officer."

"And what gives him his power?" asked Peater.

"He's our chief nut officer," Sam repeated. Then, sensing this obvious answer was somehow not enough, he added, "He decides on the strategy, he controls the budget, he can hire and fire anyone he wants."

"Ah, the perfect example of *formal power*," said Peater. "You can also think of it as title, authority, or hard power."

"Right," said Sam. "And the more formal power you have, the more you can get done."

"Is that always the case?" Peater asked. "Are there any squirrels at your company with plenty of formal power but limited ability to get things done?"

"Oh, yes," Sam said. "We have plenty of those. Take our squirrel resources manager, for example. Seriously, take him." Mary let out a big snort, but Peater looked at Sam sympathetically.

"It's tough when that happens, isn't it?" he said. "We give employees formal power with high hopes they'll use it to achieve our goals, but no one follows their lead, and nothing gets done. In the meantime, there are squirrels without any formal power who somehow manage to get everyone's respect and attention."

"Paloma!" Sam said. "There's a squirrel just like that at our company, Nuts for You. If you went by how much everyone listens to her, you'd think she was in charge."

"Ah, Paloma," said Peater, as though he knew her well. "Just the right example to help us understand *informal power*. You can also think of it as influence or soft power."

"Do you know how this Paloma of yours earned her power?" asked Alfie.

"Well, if power comes from controlling access to valuable resources . . ." Sam paused and pondered what valuable resources this low-level squirrel could possibly have. Paloma was a hard nut to crack. Then he remembered her bold voice ringing out over the nervous crowd at their last all-paws meeting. "She's always asking questions!" said Sam. "It's a pain in the tail, but it gets her and the others access to information. I guess it gives them clarity and probably a sense of security too. Those count as valuable resources, right?"

"I'd say so," said Alfie. "Most squirrels would pay a pretty peanut for clarity and safety."

"Okay, but which of the two types of power is best?" asked Sam, suddenly feeling unreasonably nervous that he'd misspent his energy chasing the wrong type of power.

"You tell me," said Peater brightly, as though Sam's whole life wasn't in question.

So, Sam thought back to Paloma. She could influence decisions, but she could not make them. Then Sam thought of Ravi. He could get compliance, but he could not get commitment. They were both all tree bark and no bite.

"Both!" Sam said. "Informal power alone takes too much work. But formal power alone is useless, especially if squirrels have other job options."

"We think so too," said Mary. "And even when there aren't other job options available, why make employees feel exploited when they can feel engaged?"

"It's why we're so deliberate about growing informal *and* formal power in our community," said Peater. "We need individuals to hold both for our collective power to grow."

"That's impossible!" Sam burst out. He thought of all the bad bosses he'd had in his career. Wasn't the worst part simply feeling stuck with them? "Informal power comes with choice, doesn't it?" he said. "When someone has formal power, you have no choice but to follow them."

"That can be true," said Mary, "but here's the thing: The only sustainable power is consensual. You can't grab power for long. You have to earn it and keep on earning it."

"And you'll only get to keep it as long as you use that power to benefit those who are granting it to you," said Dasher.

"But that's ridiculous," Sam snorted. "Employees don't grant power to their boss."

"Oh, no?" said Dasher with a knowing smile.

And this time, Sam thought of his own employees and considered for the first time that maybe, possibly, potentially he had not earned his power from them after all. Lately, when he demanded more productivity, didn't they actually produce less?

"How about dictators and tyrants and despots with absolute power?" Sam protested. "They can force everyone to do what they want no matter what anyone thinks!"

"Yep," said Dasher, "but sooner or later, individuals find a way to take their power back. And it usually doesn't turn out very well for the dictators . . . or the despots."

"Or the tyrants," said Alfie.

"So, how?" asked Sam. "Tell me how it's possible to have formal and informal power."

"Well, can you think of an example of someone who has both?" asked Peater.

Sam remembered Dasher telling them that empathetic squirrels are more likely to succeed in the workplace. So that must mean their informal power earns them their formal power and lets them keep it. But he couldn't think of anyone he knew like that. He bit into his cheek in frustration and winced in pain. And suddenly, he had the perfect example.

"My wife, Amara," Sam said to the group, and a small lump rose to his throat. "She's one of the most respected dentists in our forest. She has formal power with her staff, but they respect her because she takes the time to build informal power too. She listens to them and teaches them. I guess her patients give her power too because she uses it to help them."

"She sounds like a great leader," said Mary.

And Sam saw with a swell of sadness and love that Mary was right. All this time, Sam had thought he was the most impressive leader in their family because of how many employees he had, how much more he earned, and how much fancier his title was. But it was Amara who their pups should have been looking to as their role model. Suddenly, he felt smaller than he had been when standing beside the massive marmot earlier that day.

CHECK-IN QUESTIONS:
INFORMAL POWER

What have you noticed about informal power in your own life?

- *Think of someone who has lots of influence without formal authority. How did they earn it? How do they keep it?*

- *How about you? On a scale of 1 to 10, how much informal power do you have at work? How did you earn it? How might you grow it?*

Chapter 15

• • • • • • •

Power-Over and Power-With

"Pssst," said Mary in an exaggerated whisper. "Okay if we interrupt your existential crisis?" She tried to look serious, but Sam could see her eyes sparkle with suppressed laughter.

"We've all had one of those at some point," said Dasher. "Actually, I've had several."

"Each of us has had to unlearn what we used to believe about power and leadership and our relationships in general," said Peater.

"And, as you've seen, we're still learning every day," said Alfie.

"The good news is our power-with principles make it a lot easier to learn quickly and make better decisions along the way," said Mary.

"Power-with?" Sam asked in a voice so small, he was surprised by the sound of it.

"It's what we call our power paradigm," Dasher explained. "There's the power-over way you're probably familiar with: using power to control others as a way to get what you want."

"Know the way, and make them go your way," Sam mumbled.

"Exactly," said Dasher, as though Sam had just rattled off the most perfect example of the most terrible leadership philosophy.

"And then there's the power-with way," said Mary. "It means using your own power to grow the power in others so you can get more done together than you ever could alone."

"Like servant leadership?" Sam asked, but the squirrels shook their heads in unison.

"Most of us don't need bosses or servants," said Mary. "What we need are leaders who grow our power, which grows their power too. When we lead together, we all grow our capacity to get things done."

"And the more change and uncertainty we face, the more urgent the power-with way becomes," said Peater.

"What does that have to do with anything?" Sam asked.

The squirrels all exchanged a look Sam couldn't quite read. Then Mary said, "Sam, I think this is where we part ways with our scholarly squirrels." With that, she hopped down from the lab in the log. "*Cashew* later!" she called to Alfie, Peater, and Dasher.

"Chow for now," said Alfie.

The tiny professor and the two tall scientists waved goodbye, and Sam waved back. He watched Mary jump up onto a tree beside them and scamper all the way up to the top. So, Sam followed. He made his way up the rough bark and joined her on a long, bare branch overlooking the forest. He sat down beside her and followed her gaze.

The land beneath them split into two worlds. One was the dense forest Sam had just been inside, where the leafy trees stood tall and proud on a floor of colorful leaves. The other was an army of charred black trees that stood silent and motionless in the scorched earth. Sam was about to ask Mary what happened, but something in her shining, black eyes told him.

"This was your home," he said. And Mary nodded.

"A long time ago, it was home for me and many other creatures," she said, still looking out over the branch. "Some of us made it out before the fire took everything. Many of us didn't."

"I'm so sorry, Mary," said Sam. And they sat quietly for a while and looked out at the blackened forest together.

"We lost so much in that fire," she said at last, "but we gained something too."

"What could you possibly gain?" Sam asked, shivering at the sight of all those dead trees protruding like spikes from the ground.

"It took us a long time," said Mary, her gaze distant, as though she were watching a scene replay inside her mind. "In the midst of all that chaos and uncertainty, many of us tried to grasp power to survive. I hate to admit it, but I also had that power-over instinct. And the more tightly we clung to power, the more it seemed to dwindle. Just when we were very weak, we fought each other and became even weaker."

"That doesn't sound like anything worth gaining."

"No, it wouldn't have been," she said, "except that we learned from it. When you can learn, you can change. And when you can change, you can overcome anything. Don't you think?"

Sam thought back to his first impression of Mary's forest—that fresh, green prairie under the boundless blue sky, the fat bunches of acorns sprinkled all around.

"Did the fighting stop once you found this place?" he asked. He imagined how easy it would be to feel generous when there was abundance everywhere you looked. But Mary shook her head.

"Actually, it was the other way around. We only found this place once we found the power-with way. It's like it unlocked this ability in us to accomplish amazing things together, even with all those obstacles crashing into our path. It's what let us figure out how to adapt, even when our future looked nothing like our past. And, ultimately, it's pretty simple."

"Simple?" Sam said with undisguised skepticism.

"A lot simpler than living with the alternative," she said with a sad smile and a glance down at the burnt forest.

"Well?" said Sam. "How does it work?"

"In a nutshell?" said Mary. "The power-with way just has two parts: grow personal power, and distribute power well so it's not too concentrated in any individual or group."

"Okay. I get it," said Sam. "Give everyone power—not too little and not too much. That sounds good in principle. But how do you do it in practice?"

"I could tell you, Sam," said Mary with a familiar sparkle returning to her eyes. "But wooden you like me to show you?"

Let's take a short break here and catch our breaths before we continue. Sam just learned a lot about power, and perhaps you did too. Here is a brief summary:

- *Power is the capacity to get things done. So, having more power means having fewer limits on what we can accomplish. The more change and uncertainty we face, the more important it is to have power because it lets us reach our goals even as they change and as new obstacles emerge.*
- *Power comes from having control over access to scarce and valuable resources—especially those that increase safety or self-esteem—or the ability to take resources away.*
- *Personal power refers to the capacity of an individual.*
- *Collective power refers to the capacity of a group.*
- *To grow personal and collective capacity, we need a balance of power. If an individual has too little or too much power, the group suffers and, often, so does the individual.*
- *Sudden access to power can create feelings of uncertainty, insecurity, and isolation. When we feel a sense of social connection and support, using our power feels safer.*
- *Feeling powerful increases proactivity, creativity, and willingness to share our perspectives.*

- *Feeling powerless produces stress, inaction, withdrawal, and even health problems.*
- *Having too much power can reduce our empathy and increase our odds of taking thoughtless risks, making mistakes, and breaking rules.*
- *Formal power comes from official authority. To be sustainable, it must be granted voluntarily.*
- *Informal power comes from earning influence. Usually, you can get more accomplished when you have informal and formal power combined.*
- *Power-over refers to using power to control others or to limit their power.*
- *Power-with refers to using our personal power to increase others' power, which, in turn, increases our own. It is a way to lead together. And by lifting up the group, we ultimately lift up ourselves.*
- *The power-with way relies on two strategies: grow personal (formal and informal) power in others, and distribute power so it's not too concentrated with any person or group.*

CHECK-IN QUESTIONS

• *What else have you noticed about Mary's community and its relationship to power?*

• *Now let's talk about you—the secret hero of this story. In what ways have you leaned on a power-over approach in the past? In what ways have you practiced a power-with model? How did these choices impact you and others?*

Up next in our squirrely adventure, Sam will learn the four power-with principles and see how they play out in the workplace. We'll head deeper into the forest and deeper into the practice of leading together so you and Sam can both emerge with fresh ideas to bring back into your (squ)worlds.

Shall we continue the journey?

PART III

POWER-WITH PRINCIPLES

Chapter 16

. . . .

The Business District

Back down on the ground, Sam shook his head and scoffed at himself. He trod behind Mary and her bouncy question-mark tail as she led him toward a thicket of tall, slim trees at the edge of the open prairie. On the branch overlooking the forest, she gave him the perfect way out of this strange adventure. He could have asked her to tell him how it worked, this whole power-with way thing. But somehow, he couldn't resist having a look.

He tried to comfort himself with the thought that following Mary some more would give him another chance to find the real leader around here. Leading together, or not, someone had to have the authority to set up a trade agreement. He was determined not to go home empty-pawed. He was determined to prove to Jack Walnuts that he wasn't a phony. But the truest reason for his willingness to romp through the forest with this squirrel guide by his side was that he now felt as hungry for the secrets of this community as he had been for its acorns.

"Where are you taking me now?" Sam called to Mary just as she reached the edge of the tree-lined meadow. She twirled around and chuckled at the sight of his wary expression.

"I think you'll like it, Sam. We're going to visit our business district."

"Business district!" Sam exclaimed. "You squirrels have businesses?"

"Sure," said Mary. "Our community members have lots of different needs, so lots of different businesses pop up to fulfill them."

"But I thought you just gave everything away for free," Sam said with a nod to the clusters of unattended acorns scattered all around them.

"We never create false scarcity," she said, "but some resources are limited, so businesses spring up to exchange value for value."

Sam craned his neck back to examine the tower of trees before them. He wondered what peculiar business practices could lie within. He also wondered if this trip into the so-called business district would be a colossal waste of time. Then he took a deep breath and stepped inside.

The light and temperature changed immediately. Bright yellow and red leaves high above tinted the sunshine that fell through the treetops and cast soft shadows all around. The ground was cool beneath his feet and fallen leaves formed a thick, soft carpet that ran through the forest. Tiny leaves twirled through the air as they sailed down to the ground like a gentle rain. Before Sam had the chance to take in much more, Mary tapped him on the shoulder.

"I see just the right squirrels to show us around," she said. She hopped toward a small group perched together on a tall branch. "Sam, these are some of our community's most experienced business squirrels. Don't they say good things come in trees?"

The three squirrels looked down at Sam from their branch, so Sam waved up at them sheepishly. Mary grinned. And Sam suddenly felt like he'd swallowed a frozen acorn. What if these were the most important squirrels in town, and he'd already made an under-whelming impression? There was that unnerving sensation again: he couldn't figure out how to figure out their hierarchy. Who was perfectly fine to dismiss, and who demanded his respect and atten-tion? By the time he constructed his posture into what seemed like the right mix of deference and dominance, the squirrels were gone.

"Hello, Sam," someone said in a soft voice nearby, and Sam saw the whole group was already on the ground beside him. "I'm Robin Walnut Karrier," said a fox squirrel with a thick, gray-gold coat and kind eyes. "And if you're wondering why my paws are so muddy, it's because my team and I have a gardening company."

"I'm Ricardo Seedler," said a dark red flying squirrel with a long, thin tail he rested on his own shoulder. "I have an engineering company that serves our community's safety needs."

"And I'm Adam Pomogrant," said a blue-eyed prairie dog.

"He helps the rest of us stay in business," said Ricardo with a crooked smile.

"I hope so," said Adam. "I apply my research to consult our local businesses."

"We're sorry to interrupt," said Mary. "I was just hoping you might help me show Sam some of our power-with principles in the workplace."

"No apology necessary," said Robin, wiping the fresh earth from her paws on a large yellow leaf. "I bet we could all use a break. We were just sharing the biggest business mistakes each of us made in the past week. It makes for great learning—"

"And laughing," Ricardo added.

"Did you say you were confessing your mistakes to each other?" Sam repeated. In his High Tails leadership club back home, the members would never have displayed their weaknesses willingly. Sure, they complained about their staff, their board, or their customers, but it was with the implicit understanding that these were problems outside their control. And when they were not complaining, they were showing off, bragging, judging, or asking for business referrals.

"I wouldn't say we were confessing mistakes, would you?" Adam asked the group with a glimmer in his bright blue eyes.

"Maybe more like reporting," said Robin.

"Or regaling," said Ricardo, and the others chuckled.

"We try to make it a habit around here to talk about our mistakes," said Mary in response to Sam's pained expression. "It helps us learn faster."

"Plus it keeps our egos in check," said Ricardo.

"And some of us need that more than others," said Robin with a playful punch on Ricardo's shoulder. He gasped in mock dismay and brushed off a speck of dirt she left on his shiny, red fur.

"But how could your employees trust you afterward?" asked Sam, feeling a touch appalled by where this conversation was headed.

"We're not suggesting you walk around talking about your mistakes all day," said Ricardo. "Your team would like to know you're competent too—if you are, in fact, competent."

"But they also need to know you're listening and learning," said Adam. "When you show you've learned from bad decisions in the past, it helps others trust you'll make good decisions in the future. Besides, it also strengthens your team. My colleague and I found that when leaders tell others about negative feedback they've received, it increases their team's sense of safety."[16]

"Can you think of anyone who's shared their mistakes with you?" asked Robin.

Sam thought about it. As good a leader as he now knew Amara was, she did not make a habit of talking about her mistakes—at least not at home. Sam certainly never heard Jack Walnuts acknowledge where he went wrong either. (And he very much hoped his first admission would *not* be his mistake promoting Sam.) Then Sam's gaze landed on Mary.

Back there on the long branch far above the forest, she had told him about the fire that obliterated her home and the fear and anger that made everyone, herself included, cling to power. Sam hadn't realized it until now, but something shifted in him after that conversation. Despite all her strange quirks and *acorny* puns, he couldn't help but trust her now. What's more, he also found it easier now to try on new ways of thinking. By sharing her moment of weakness, Mary somehow made it feel safer for him to take risks. He caught her gaze and smiled, and she smiled in return.

"Yes," said Sam. "I can think of someone like that."

"Good, good," said Ricardo, "and we'll also tell you all sorts of things we've done wrong. But how about we start with the power-with principles we're pretty sure we've gotten right?"

"Please do," said Sam. Ricardo draped his long, red tail over Sam's shoulder and grinned.

"What do you say to paying Robin's team a visit first?" he asked the group. "Isn't today the perfect day to illustrate the first principle?"

"First principle?"

"The power-with way has four principles," Mary explained. "Each one helps us make better decisions about how we use power."

"Good thinking," said Robin. "I'll tell you a brief story[17] before I explain the first principle."

Chapter 17

. . . .

Bad Medicine: Robin's Story

Before I started my company, I was a pharmacologist at a clinic very far from here, in more ways than one. It was hard work, but I loved my job. I got to forage all day in the woods, picking out the plumpest mushrooms and the most fragrant wild roots and herbs. In the evenings, I brought armfuls of ingredients back to my cozy lab and made medicines for our patients. I rarely got to see the squirrels I was helping, but every night I went to bed, snug with the belief that I was making their lives better.

One day, the owner of the clinic called everyone into her office. Her red fur looked even redder than usual, and she was hopping mad.

"Do you know how low our clinic rating is for the third quarter in a row?" she demanded. Nobody answered because I don't think anyone knew what our rating was or how it got there. Somewhere in the back of my mind, I always figured it was important but, even more important, none of my business. Eventually, the silence stretched so long someone said, "Too low?"

"You're dogwood right it's too low!" our boss shouted and got even redder. "And if we want to keep our clinic open and our jobs safe, we'd better improve our reputation and do it quickly."

After that meeting, there was so much panic in the air, even our patients felt it. I couldn't imagine what would happen to them and their families if our clinic closed, but I didn't know how to help. So, I just started going around and asking questions. That's how I learned the rumor that squirrels often left our clinic feeling worse than when they came in. I was so rattled, I stayed up all night checking and rechecking my medicines. I couldn't find anything wrong.

But the next day, I stumbled onto the root of the problem. I happened to be at the front desk dropping off a new batch of medicine when I heard one of the clinic's star doctors barking orders at a nurse.

"Three sassafras leaves?" the nurse repeated.

"That's what I said," said the doctor and walked off without another word. The nurse sighed and plucked a bright yellow petal off a sassafras flower.

"Excuse me," I said, leaning over the counter, "but isn't that the wrong dose to treat an infection?"

"That's what I thought too," the nurse said and proceeded to pluck two more petals.

"But that many petals can make someone sick!"

"Look," said the nurse, "I appreciate your concern, but the last time I tried to question a doctor, I got my tail handed to me and my hours cut. They've made it very clear my job here is to follow orders. We just have to hope they know what they're doing."

I couldn't stop shaking after that exchange. The very medicines I made with such care and concern for our patients were turning into poisons in the paws of overconfident doctors who couldn't tolerate getting their egos bruised by someone lower than them on the hospital hierarchy. I ran straight to the owner's office and let her know what was happening. I was sure if we could get our doctors to take feedback from our nurses, we could help our patients and maybe our clinic too.

"So you're saying you want the nurses to question the doctors' authority?" she said.

"If it's in the best interest of our patients," I answered.

"Then I suppose you also think it's okay for you to march in here and question *my* authority and how I run this clinic?" she said, and her fiery fur seemed to glow brighter.

"If it's in the best interest of our patients," I said again.

And that's how I lost my job. She said something about me not being a culture fit and told me to pack up my things and go. I left that very same day, but the experience stayed with me forever. I decided right then and there to start my own company doing something different and doing it differently.

I promised myself I'd do everything in my power to keep our purpose bigger than any one person, myself included—to make our *why* more important than any *who*. Without knowing it at the time, I figured out the first principle of the power-with way.

Chapter 18

Principle #1: Follow a Purpose, Not a Person

"Which is . . . ?" Sam asked Robin, feeling eager and restless at the same time.

"Follow a purpose, not a person."

"Huh?" said Sam.

"Come see for yourself," said Robin. And with that, she took off, and the others followed.

The squirrels raced so quickly through the colorful forest that Sam barely had time to take in his surroundings. All sorts of bustling shops flashed by, from fruit and flower vendors to a dance studio to a pup-sitting service and many others he couldn't categorize. Through the cheerful crunch of leaves underfoot, Sam could hear snatches of chatter, laughter, and even singing.

Ricardo glided before them on his dark red squirrel wings and reached their destination first. Adam popped up shortly after from an underground tunnel and shook the soil off his light coat. Sam ran with the tree squirrels and panted as he came to a full stop behind

Mary, Robin, and their bushy tails. Robin motioned to the group to be quiet. She slipped inside a cavernous opening in a giant tree. The others followed, and Sam carefully slid in after them.

Inside, a group of squirrels sat atop thick roots that snaked through the dim cave in the tree. They burst into applause just as Sam entered, and he froze. Then, to his relief, he realized the applause was not for them. A short, striped chipmunk cleared his throat and raised his paw.

"I can go next," he said, and the group murmured their encouragement. "The garden you planted for our family saved my son's life," he said. And the room grew still. "Our pup was sick for a long time, and we were losing hope. But all those bright flowers and butterflies outside our window gave him something to look forward to each day. And once our little garden came alive, so did countless other plants and creatures all around us. You didn't just plant flowers for us, you planted hope." He lowered his head in gratitude, and, again, applause erupted from the group.

"Is this some kind of support group?" Sam whispered. But Robin shook her head.

"Once a month, we have our customers stop by to tell us how we've impacted their lives," she said. "It's what reminds us of our purpose, why we do what we do every day."

"It's one thing to understand that your work has meaning, but it's a whole other thing to see it for yourself," said Adam, his blue eyes shining in the dim light. "Our research shows hearing directly from the individuals your work impacts can improve employee performance by 400 percent."[18]

"Four hundred percent!" Sam shouted. And the entire group turned to look at him. Mary covered his mouth and shoved him back out of the tree, giggling the entire time. Robin, Adam, and Ricardo followed them, looking similarly amused.

"Yep," said Adam once they got back outside. "We consistently see an increase in the effort individuals put in and the results they get out when they see their work has real purpose. But it's not some ploy to crank up productivity. It's a fundamental paradigm shift in how we work and lead together."

"That's why it's the first principle of the power-with way," said Robin. "Follow a purpose, not a person."

"I still don't get it," said Sam. "How can you have a company without a person in charge?"

"It's not that we don't have leaders here," said Robin. "It's that we always remember our shared purpose matters more than anyone's personal preference, authority, or ego. Sorry, Ricardo," she added with a grin, and he rolled his eyes.

"We like to think of purpose as our invisible leader," said Mary.

"I guess I can see why it's motivating to know your work has purpose," said Sam, realizing his own staff never heard directly from their customers. "But how does it grow your power?"

"Remember your definition of power as the capacity to get things done?" said Mary. "Feeling inspired by the purpose of your work helps you get more done.[19] But there's a lot more to it than that. When we're clear and aligned on what we want to get done, it lets us take action without having to wait for someone to tell us what to do. It's the ultimate micromanagement buster."

"So what's the purpose of your company?" Sam asked Robin.

"To foster mutual flourishing between all living beings in our forest," she said without skipping a beat. "We plant gardens to brighten our customers' lives. And they, in turn, support biodiversity, which improves the lives of all the creatures here."

"Well, that's not fair," scoffed Sam. Then seeing Robin's bemused expression, he added, "It's easy to get behind an inspiring company mission. But what if you have a meaningless business?"

"If you have a meaningless business, you probably shouldn't be in business," said Ricardo with a smirk. "Doesn't your company have a purpose?"

"Well, yes," said Sam. He knew Nuts for You had a corporate mission statement. It was something about market dominance and superior quality, but Sam could never remember it. For a long time now, his personal purpose was to simply grow the business. But for what? To bring more wealth to himself and the company shareholders? That was just a consequence of fulfilling the company's purpose. So, what was the real purpose? To pick and distribute nuts? That purpose was right there in the company name. But was that their purpose, or just something they did? Then Sam thought of the condo development, and his stomach seemed to flip upside down. The forest recession was scary because it threatened his company's ability to achieve its purpose, didn't it? It threatened his branch, his job, and his entire family. And then it hit him.

"To feed the squirrels in our forest," Sam said. "That's our company's purpose."

"That sounds like a very important purpose," said Robin as she placed one golden paw on his. "Do you notice how different it feels to serve that purpose rather than a person?"

Sam considered it. All this time, Jack Walnuts and his gruff voice and wildfire tail loomed largest in his mind. Sam was accountable only to him. What would it be like to be accountable to a mission instead of a manager?

"I think I see," said Sam. "It's more uplifting and a lot clearer."

"Exactly," said Adam. "When we follow one shared purpose, it gives us the power to make progress faster toward the same goal."

"On the flip side," said Ricardo, "when you follow a person above a purpose, it slows down progress while everyone waits for orders. I don't know about you, but we don't have patience to move at that pace."

Sam wanted to argue, but deep down he already knew Ricardo was right. He remembered complaining to the High Tails that his staff didn't do anything he didn't tell them to. He had always assumed the problem was them. But what if he was the bottleneck to their progress because he left them with no power to take action in the absence of his orders? Had he been so busy trying to know the way and make them go his way that he actually came to stand in their way?

"And, of course, a lack of progress isn't even the worst thing that happens when you prioritize a person over a purpose," said Robin with a shiver. "That kind of power-over thinking permeated my clinic and ended up hurting everyone involved." Sam considered if his own power-over antics had kept squirrels from speaking up if he ever made a decision that put the branch in danger, and a cloud of dread darkened in his mind.

"It's okay," said Robin as she patted his paw again. "We're all still learning."

"I guess I do have some learning to do," said Sam, "but I still don't understand. Can you tell me how you put the first principle into practice?"

"We can *tail* you all about it," said Mary. "It comes back to the two power-with strategies: grow personal power, and distribute power well."

Just then, squirrels began filing out of the cave in the tree. Some smiled, some wiped tears from their eyes, and some patted one another on the back.

"As you can see," said Adam, "our personal power is fueled when we get to see the impact of our work with our own eyes. It gives us the energy and clarity we need to keep going."

"But there's more," said Ricardo. "Watch this." And he flew over to a ground squirrel exiting the tree and said, "Hey there! Would you do us a favor and tell us your company mission?"

"Uh, sure," said the squirrel with a surprised but friendly smile. "We foster mutual flourishing between all living beings in our forest."

"And how do you achieve that purpose?" asked Ricardo.

"Well, our company strategy is to plant gardens that benefit squirrels directly and attract pollinators who help more plants grow, which benefits all creatures indirectly," said the squirrel. "So, our objective this year is to increase our number of gardens by 30 percent from last year. And our priority is to plant more small gardens, even over a smaller number of large gardens. That way we can reach more pollinators and recruit more customers who become fans of gardens."

"Thanks very much," said Ricardo, and the squirrel shrugged, smiled, and walked off.

"Was that one of your executives?" asked Sam, already fantasizing about how much easier his job would be with that squirrel on his management team.

"That was one of our newest gardeners," said Robin. "Every member of our team knows our purpose, strategy, goals, and priorities, so they have the personal power to make good decisions without waiting for someone to tell them what to do."

"And there's something else," said Ricardo coyly. He hopped over to two chipmunks chatting by the base of the giant tree. "I beg your pardon," he said. "Would you please tell us the purpose of your roles?"[20] The chipmunks looked up blinking.

"Sure," said the smaller chipmunk. "The purpose of my role is to increase awareness of our company so more squirrels are interested in having a garden. About one in five squirrels knows about us now, so my goal this quarter is to increase that number to one in four."

"These days, the purpose of my role is to make sure we always know our expenses so we can afford to keep improving the quality of our gardens," said the other chipmunk. "This month, I'm helping reduce our bookkeeping time from twelve hours a month to six hours so we can make financial decisions faster." Ricardo flashed them a big smile, and the chipmunks resumed their conversation.

"I think I get it," said Sam. "Power comes from understanding the purpose of your company and role. Instead of waiting for some person to lead the way, you're able to lead together."

"Yes," said Robin, "and having definitions of success gives everyone the power to assess their own progress, instead of just relying on others to tell them how they're doing. We still value feedback, but the most meaningful feedback tends to come from results you can measure yourself."

"Okay fine," said Sam. "I understand how following a purpose before a person can grow personal power. But how does the first principle help you distribute power so it doesn't get too concentrated?"

"Look who's paying attention!" Ricardo exclaimed, and Sam blushed under his gray coat.

"I suspect you might already know, Sam," said Adam, watching Sam intently with his piercing blue eyes. "What have you noticed around here so far?"

So, Sam thought back to his adventures since that morning. What was it these squirrels did to keep power with the purpose rather than the person? Who were their powerful persons, anyway? Based on the position of the sun over the glowing yellow and red treetops, Sam guessed it was about eleven o'clock. Hours had passed since he woke up in their community this morning. And yet, he was no closer to figuring out who was really in charge. He realized this must be his answer.

"Power isn't concentrated with anyone here," he said. "In fact, no one seems to be the most important . . . anything."

"Ouch," said Ricardo, and Robin gave him a small slap on the arm.

"I mean, I can see you do have important experts with authority to lead work and make decisions," said Sam, "but they seem to be as approachable as anyone else."

"Nice save," said Ricardo.

"How do you think we manage to do that?" asked Adam, ignoring the flying squirrel.

"Well, you all seem to be allergic to any kind of status symbols," said Sam, still feeling a little annoyed by it but seeing now that it's what made him treat everyone with more respect. "You don't have fancy titles or offices. And you're always ready to make fun of each other."[21]

"Only when we deserve it," said Ricardo.

"You share your mistakes openly," Sam went on, "so everyone seems fallible instead of perfect. I can see how it lets you learn faster, but I suppose it also keeps any one squirrel from coming across as too powerful."

"That's right," said Adam. "It also helps that everyone plays a role in interviewing and selecting the individuals who have formal authority to impact them."

"You mean employees get to hire their own bosses?" Sam nearly shouted.

"Yes, and assess how well they're doing too," said Robin.

"But that's nuts," said Sam. "Wouldn't I just complain about any boss who made me work hard and hire a boss who let me coast?"

"Not if you had a shared purpose," said Mary. "Remember, we only grant power to someone when we believe they can use it to benefit us. So, Dasher leads the lab because he's so good at helping reach its purpose of making discoveries about power. Robin leads her company because her team believes she can help them achieve biodiversity."

"And what if nobody cares about a purpose that's any higher than getting paid?" said Sam.

"Well, most of us want more than just payment," said Robin, "but even if that's not the case, then as long as employees earn more money when their company makes money, then they'll give power to individuals who are good at increasing profitability."

Sam scratched his chin and thought it over. He liked the idea of Mr. Walnuts admitting his mistakes, giving up his shiny duplex office, and asking Sam for feedback on his leadership. But would Sam be willing to do the same himself?

"How do you convince squirrels to give up their power?" he asked.

"It's not about passing power from one squirrel to the next," said Robin. "It's about sharing power with others so there's more of it for everyone. It's about achieving mutual flourishing."

CHECK-IN QUESTIONS: FOLLOW A PURPOSE, NOT A PERSON

Let's examine the first principle of the power-with way a bit more closely before we move on:

- Think of a time you or others prioritized a person over a purpose (e.g., avoided giving feedback or challenging authority or chose to please a person rather than doing what's best for the purpose). What could have made it easier to follow the purpose?

- On a scale of 1–10, how clear are your company (1) purpose _____, (2) strategy _____, (3) objectives _____, and (4) priorities _____? How about on your team (1) purpose _____, (2) success metrics _____, and (3) priorities _____? How about your role (1) purpose_____, (2) success metrics _____, and (3) priorities _____? How might you increase that score?

"Okay, okay," said Sam (though he wasn't sure yet if he was actually okay with this first principle). "Follow a purpose, not a person. Got it. What's principle number two?"

"Shall we visit Ricardo's office to chat about that?" said Robin with a little jab at the flying squirrel's side.

"Oh, I see what's going on here," said Ricardo. "You all won't be content until I've fully discredited myself in front of our guest. Very well, then. Let's get this over with."

Without another word, Ricardo jumped up onto a stocky tree and parachuted to the next one and the next. The others followed, except for Adam, who traveled underground. Sam expected the group to lead him back to the colorful center of the business district, but, to his surprise, they leapt into the denser, darker part of the forest that grew down a steep hill. The air turned cooler, the light dimmer, and soon Sam could barely hear the chipper sounds of squirrels they left behind. Everywhere he looked, thick, dry vines snaked up and draped down from the trees. Finally, Ricardo landed on a large, dead tree that seemed to have taken a trust fall into the arms of the nearby trees.

"I'll tell you the second power-with principle," he said, "but let me give you a bit of backstory first."

Chapter 19

· · · · · · ·

Ash Trees: Ricardo's Story

A long time ago, in a forest far, far away, there was a handsome flying squirrel who had everything figured out. He ran a successful business providing winter homes high up in the tallest, strongest ash trees in the forest. His scouts scoured high and low to find the coziest spots for squirrels to spend the season. Demand was so high, the company had clients on a waitlist.

This strapping squirrel had a crystal clear vision for his company, and he made sure everyone who worked for him followed it exactly. There was a long list of company rules for everything from precisely how high above the ground the nests must be (thirty feet) to how long the lunch breaks were allowed to be (thirty minutes). It was all wonderfully, perfectly predictable until . . . it wasn't. The scouts tried to tell their leader something was wrong.

"The ash bark doesn't look right," they said in one meeting.

"Branches keep crashing down without warning," they told him at the next meeting.

But their leader didn't want to hear it. In fact, his orders became even stricter and his list of rules even longer. In the meantime, his clients grew nervous, and his waitlist vanished. But it wasn't until a family nearly died when the tree that held their new home collapsed that he finally understood there was a crisis. It turned out that small, emerald insects were finding their way into the bark of the ash trees and leaving these great giants lifeless.

I wish I could tell you this strapping squirrel was as wise as he was handsome. But, alas, this wasn't the case. At first, he actually doubled down on his rules and told his scouts to find him more healthy ash trees faster. They insisted the emerald bugs would get to them too, but their brash boss told them to stop asking questions and start following orders.

To their credit, many of them told him to kiss their ash and left. Pretty soon, so did most of the company's clients. So, the flying squirrel and his remaining team went deeper into the forest, looking for a place where the ash trees were still strong. Instead, they were lucky enough to wander into this community.

As you might have noticed, the folks around here like to ask lots of questions. They asked the flying squirrel and his scouts why they were so determined to build homes in ash trees when there were other kinds of trees around. The scouts couldn't answer and just turned to look at their leader. Only then did he realize he'd never actually explained the reasons behind his rules. And as he learned more about the nature of power, he understood that no matter how powerful his vision might be, he was building a powerless team.

The following week, he brought together the small group of employees who remained at his company and the pawful of clients who hadn't yet given up on them.

"Did you know ash trees can live for hundreds of years?" he told them. "Our clients could pass down their nests from generation to generation. They could enjoy the safety and stability I never had when I was growing up. Ever since I was a pup, I promised myself I'd build ash tree homes for all the families who needed them."

"I understand," said his most tenured employee. "I also grew up without a warm, dry place to call home." Several other squirrels in the group nodded.

"How strange that we never knew that," said the leader.

"I guess we never asked."

After that, they all went around and asked questions and learned about each other's hopes and fears for the business. Their leader even managed to explain the reasons behind his many (many) rules.

"It looks like we all want the same thing," said one of the clients, "but could it be there's another way to achieve it?"

Everything started to change after that meeting—slowly at first, then faster and faster. Once the scouts had sufficient context, they could move quickly and make informed and creative decisions. They had a sense of freedom and ownership over their own work. And, best of all, they had the power to find a better solution.

Chapter 20

Principle #2: Rely on Context, Not Control

"So did they?" asked Sam. "Did they figure out a solution once you gave them the context?" He couldn't bear to keep listening to this story unfold. It sounded much too much like a preview of his own life once the humans brought their machines into the forest to build their condo.

"Ah, I see you identified the hapless hero of my story," said Ricardo. And then he patted the dead tree beneath him. "You're looking at the solution, Sam."

"A dead tree?" said Sam.

"I beg your pardon," said Ricardo. "This dead tree happens to house our company headquarters. I can see you're impressed!" he added and bowed with a flourish.

Sam glanced at the other squirrels to see if they looked impressed, because he certainly wasn't. He thought back to his own branch office—that towering, ancient oak he'd known all his life, and his tail straightened with pride.

"You could have *spruced* it up a bit," said Mary.

"I think it's beautiful just the way it is," said Robin.

"I think so too," said Ricardo. "But I never would have noticed it if it weren't for my team. You see, I always told my scouts to find the tallest, healthiest trees in the sunniest parts of the forest. But once they had enough context and the freedom to make decisions, they figured out it's the fallen ash trees in the densest parts of the forest that now make the best homes. The dead trees can't get any deader, and all those vines we used to treat as threats catch falling branches so they can't hurt anyone down below."

"Wow," said Sam. And only then did he notice they were surrounded by dozens of fallen ash trees, with their distinctive ashy bark and diamond pattern of their ridges and furrows.

"Yep," said Ricardo. "They're not the most glamorous homes, but they're the safest, and that's what matters to our clients. Ever since we've understood that, we've engineered all sorts of new solutions to create more safety for them." Sam looked around at the dark, tree-crammed forest with new admiration. What seemed to him like a wasteland at first now felt more like a wonderland. "And none of this would be possible if I hadn't learned the most important leadership lesson of my life," said Ricardo.

"Which is?" asked Sam.

"The second principle of the power-with way!"

"Well, it's about time," said Sam. To his relief, the others laughed.

"Right?" said Robin. "He's gotten much better at sharing power, this one. But when he gets a chance to do all the talking, he still takes it."

"Only because I'm so good at it," said Ricardo.

"The second principle of the power-with way is this," said Adam, mercifully getting back to the point. "*Rely on context, not control.*"

"Rely on context, not control," Sam repeated, trying to make sense of it.

"Yep," said Ricardo. "Just about everything about the way I tried to lead my company relied on taking control. I was the host of the classic power-over party. I kept all the formal power to myself and used it to tell everyone *what* to do instead of *why* we do it. We had a shared purpose, but I didn't give them any of the context or freedom they needed to achieve it. Any time I didn't like what someone was doing, I created another rule. I even had a rule about memorizing all our rules."

"And all your team needed to become successful was to understand the context behind your vision?" asked Sam.

"I wish," Ricardo snorted. "But relying on context instead of control requires a constant dedication to sharing power. Now, I like to think I've transformed from a control freak into a context freak."

"What do you mean by constant dedication?" asked Sam.

"Well, it means I'm always sharing important information with everyone on my team and checking to make sure they've understood it," said Ricardo. "Every time I make a request or give someone feedback, I share my reasoning and ask others to do it too. I can't tell you how many times a day I say, 'And the reasoning is' or, 'The context behind this is.'"

"That sounds simple enough," said Sam.

"It also means I've scrapped any business speak that can get in the way of someone's understanding," said Ricardo, "or of revealing I don't know what I'm talking about."

Sam gulped. This last bit sounded a little harder. He was so used to spitting out business jargon to cover up his insecurities, it seemed unthinkable to strip away all that protection. And how on earth would he manage to be impressive without his impressive vocabulary?

"Okay," he said, eager to move on to another topic, "sharing context grows personal power because it gives you the information you need to take action and make good decisions. And it's a lot more motivating than feeling controlled.[22] But how does it reduce power concentration?"

"Oh, that part is my favorite," said Ricardo. "Remember the long list of rules I told you I had? Well, not only was I the designated rule writer, but I was also our one and only approver."

"What's wrong with that?" said Sam, getting preemptively defensive.

"You tell me," said Ricardo. And, in a flash, Sam saw an entire montage of requests he had to bring to Mr. Walnuts for his approval. Any time he wanted to take a day off, come in late, work from home, or buy something for the branch, he had to ask for permission. Maybe it made sense for large purchases or major policy changes, but did Sam really need his boss's permission for everything? How much time and frustration could they have saved if Sam had more formal power to make decisions?

"Fine," said Sam, "I can see how having a long list of rules and a small number of approvers could slow things down, but I don't see any way around it."

"I couldn't either at first," said Ricardo. "So, I took the challenge to my team, and we got our long list of rules down to just three: before you make a decision, (1) understand the context, (2) use your best judgment, (3) ask for feedback."

"But how can you trust them not to take advantage of your company?" said Sam.

"It's a funny sort of math," said Ricardo. "It turns out the cost of a few folks taking advantage tends to be much lower than the cost of everyone feeling controlled."

"And when you trust someone, they usually become more trustworthy," said Robin.

"Even if everything you're saying is true," said Sam, "isn't it still a waste of time—having everyone hash out every decision instead of just following some simple rules?"

"Sometimes," said Ricardo. "But the risk of underthinking tends to be higher than the risk of overthinking, especially when there's so much change and uncertainty around."

"Besides, your employees can always create guidelines together when it makes sense to do so," said Robin, "as long as they have the authority to change them when they stop being helpful."

"I also thought it was totally nuts at first," said Ricardo, apparently guessing Sam's thoughts. "Then again, the old me would find just about everything about the way we work today totally nuts. I might still be resisting all this change if it wasn't for the one, tiny, hard-to-ignore fact that it works."

Sam mulled over everything he'd just heard and considered his own situation. Had he shared any context at all with his staff back at the branch? He hadn't told them about the condo development. He hadn't explained why he was increasing their nut-gathering quota. For that matter, neither had Jack Walnuts. Sam had given them neither information nor authority to come up with creative solutions to their imminent condo-development problem. But could he really trust them to make decisions on their own?

CHECK-IN QUESTIONS: RELY ON CONTEXT, NOT CONTROL

Let's carve out a few minutes now to contemplate the second principle of the power-with way.

- *Think of a time when you had to get things done without enough context. How did it feel? What could have helped?*

- *How might you make context clearer and more accessible for your team (e.g., share your reasoning, make information easy to access and understand, check for alignment)?*

- *What are some ways you might limit your use of control by relying more on context (e.g., reduce or eliminate rules, minimize need for approval, grant decision-making authority)?*

"I think I understand how context can produce better results than control," Sam said, "but I don't think you understand what it's like at my company. I wish our squirrels just needed context to make good decisions, but we haven't been able to find enough squirrels who can do that. There's a talent shortage in our forest."

"Ah, the old talent-shortage problem," said Ricardo with a wink. "Sounds like he's ready to learn about the third principle." Robin nodded thoughtfully and peered up into the sky beyond the dense treetops.

"Isn't it nearly time for rehearsal?" she asked Adam, and a sly smile spread across his face.

"It sure is," he said. "Would you like to see our little show, Sam?"

"I should really get back soon," said Sam.

"We can make it a quick visit," Adam promised. "In fact, I know a shortcut." And he rolled over a small log on the ground, waved to Ricardo, and disappeared into a tunnel hidden beneath it.

"This is where we say goodbye," said Ricardo from his perch atop his fallen tree. "Some of us have a waitlist of clients to tend to."

"*Cedar* later!" Mary shouted as she flew down the chute in the ground. Robin followed. So, Sam waved goodbye, held his breath, and jumped.

To his (immense) relief, the tunnel was roomier than he expected. Daylight streamed in from several openings above them and seemed to transform into golden moonbeams that spilled into the tunnels. The scent of rich, fresh soil and young tree roots filled his nose. The only unnerving sensation Sam had was the sudden quiet. There was no swirling of wind, no chirping of birds or insects, no rustling or crunching of leaves. Sam couldn't hear anything but the sound of his own breath. But before he could panic, Mary's voice called out from somewhere far ahead.

"You coming, Sam?" came her teasing tone. "I thought you said you had to get back soon."

"I'm right behind you!" Sam shouted into the tunnel and bolted ahead at full speed. As he ran, small chambers appeared on either side, some packed with freshly cut grass, some bustling with a family of prairie dogs. In one chamber, a group of rambunctious pups cheered Sam on as though he were in a race. It made him miss Remi and Josie terribly, so he ran even faster, promising himself he'd be a better leader for them, if for no other reason.

"This way!" Mary's voice rang out from the left. So, Sam made a sharp left turn and nearly fell backward in surprise. Mary, Robin, and Adam stood at the entrance to a massive cavern, nearly empty but large enough to fit an audience of one hundred squirrels. A stage rose up from the ground, and sunshine poured across it through a skylight. A groundhog was center stage, gesturing and whispering something to a cluster of squirrels in the wings.

"What is this place?" Sam whispered.

"Just the most *poplar* show in town," said Mary.

"It's our very own underground saloon," said Adam. "It's hopping with squirrels at night, but right now, the performers are rehearsing."

"Rehearsing for what?" asked Sam.

"For a magic show," said Adam with a giddy flash in his blue eyes.

"Believe it or not, before Adam helped us do magic within our businesses, he was an actual magician," said Robin, getting up on her toes to pat Adam on the shoulder.

Sam must have scrunched up his face into a dubious expression because Adam grinned and said, "I'm afraid it's true. And I have magic to thank for finding this community. I'll explain the third principle, but let me tell you a quick story about it first."

Chapter 21

• • • • • • •

Making Magic: Adam's Story

I left my colony when I was just a teenager because I knew, even as a pup, I didn't belong. I wasn't a good tunneler or fighter or forager. But I didn't know what I could do or where I should go. So, I wandered through fields and forests, doing odd jobs and feeling lost in every sense of the word. Then, one cold, rainy night, I stumbled into an empty burrow for shelter. Or at least, I thought it was empty. But a groundhog appeared before me so suddenly, I could have sworn she materialized out of thin air.

"Welcome," she said. "I'm Carol Dweckdini. Shall we begin?"

"Begin what?" I asked.

"The magician audition," she said, as though it were the most obvious reply.

"I think there's been a mistake," I said. "I'm not here for a magician audition. I can't do magic. Actually, I can't do much of anything at all."

She examined me for a while with her dark, intelligent eyes. My coat was cold and damp, and I shivered all over. I smelled like a wet prairie dog. I couldn't have looked less impressive if I tried. But a smile spread across her face, and she said, "Yet."

"Yet?"

"You can't do magic *yet*," she said. "But it's a skill like any other.[23] If you're willing to put in the effort, my team and I can teach you. Then, if you'd like, you can audition for our show."

I don't know what possessed me to say yes, but I agreed. I assisted the troop by day, and by night I watched them perform, and I practiced. I was terrible at it at first. I made so many mistakes that I was ready to quit after a month. But Carol told me magic is like a muscle we build with practice, so I kept on practicing. My magic muscles grew stronger and, pretty soon, I was good enough to perform in the show. Seeing the joy and wonder on all those faces, trusting my troop and knowing they trusted me too—it was the first time in my life I really felt I belonged.

The only problem was that our magic show was very small. Carol shared all the show's earnings with the members of the troop, but it wasn't enough for most of them to live on, especially if they had families to support. Many of them had no choice but to find other jobs, so the team put me in charge of hiring new magicians.

At first, I was so excited to give someone the kind of opportunity Carol gave me. But I quickly realized that hiring even a single magician was no easy feat.

"I'm trying as hard as I can to find us talented performers," I complained to Carol one evening, "but maybe they just don't exist." She studied me with that curious, attentive gaze of hers and smiled.

"Yet," she said.

That's when I realized how limited my thinking had been. I started to hold free classes for ground squirrels outside our troop, giving anyone who wanted a chance to grow their magic muscles and audition for the show if they liked. I taught them juggling, card tricks, and even some mentalism. Our candidate pipeline began to grow, but it still wasn't enough. So, we took our show on the road and began to recruit squirrels from different parts of the forest. It's how we came across this community.

The prairie dogs and groundhogs here welcomed us with open paws. And, to my surprise, other kinds of squirrels started asking if they could audition too. We built this theater we're in now with a skylight entrance large enough for all sorts of squirrels to use.[24] Before we knew it, our variety of acts expanded, and so did our audience. We were finally able to pay our performers a great wage.

Watching our show grow was so amazing, it made me want to help other organizations grow too. I wanted to become an organizational psychologist and maybe even a business advisor. But I had no experience in either of those fields.

"Yet," Carol reminded me when I confided in her about my dream. "Experience only comes from experience, you know," she added.

"But I can't leave the troop," I said, "not after you invested so much time and effort into my development." And as usual she just looked at me and smiled.

"When you're ready to go, others will grow into the space you leave behind," she said. And as you can see for yourself, she was right.

Chapter 22

Principle #3: Be a Cultivator, Not a Collector

Adam looked up at the sunlit stage with a bittersweet expression in his blue eyes. Sam followed his gaze and saw that the groundhog, who must have been Carol, and her troop were now rehearsing their act. They all stood in a tidy line, with Carol at the start. She plucked out a large carrot from what looked to be thin air. She held it up to the light, where it glowed bright orange. Then, she popped the entire thing in her mouth and gulped it down as though she were a snake. The line of squirrels seemed to ripple, and the last squirrel in line—a tiny chipmunk—sneezed. A carrot appeared to shoot out of his nose and flew into the audience. The little chipmunk looked embarrassed, but the groundhog just laughed and signaled to everyone to try again. So once again, a carrot emerged, vanished, and reappeared—without shooting off stage—over and over until the act looked seamless.

"There's the third principle of the power-with way in action," said Adam.

"Oh, right!" said Sam, realizing he had completely forgotten why he was there. "The third principle. Er . . . what is it exactly?"

"*Be a cultivator, not a collector,*" said Adam.

"Be a what?" asked Sam.

"A cultivator," said Robin. "Like a gardener. See, most companies try to collect employees from a small, finite crop of talent rather than cultivate an infinite field. They think skills have to be found instead of made. They search for perfect fits and never find enough of them."

"And when there's a problem, they assume they need to replace the person rather than take a good hard look at the situation," said Mary.

"If Carol only hired squirrels who already had all the knowledge they needed for the job, her magic show would be in big trouble," said Adam, nodding toward the groundhog.

This time, she and her troop were rehearsing an elaborate acorn juggling act. At first, acorns slipped out of the squirrels' paws and bounced away. Sounds of laughter, groans, and forehead slaps drifted over from the stage. But little by little, the group began to throw and catch in such synchrony that acorns seemed to levitate in the space between them.

"Whatever your company's type of magic is, you'll hold it back if you don't amplify the power that comes from expanding intrapersonal and interpersonal capabilities," said Adam.

"Intra what?" asked Sam.

"The power to get things done alone and together," said Robin. "See how each squirrel needs to learn to juggle well on their own and also together?" Sam nodded as he watched the acorns sail past one another. He had often thought about the importance of individual skills, but it never really occurred to him that his staff needed a whole other set of skills to work together well.

"That kind of informal power feels great to have," said Adam, "and it also fuels your company's ability to achieve results and adapt quickly, especially in times of change."

"Okay, okay, you don't have to convince me of this principle," said Sam. "I'd love to get our squirrels to learn new skills. The problem is they don't want to learn."

"They don't want to learn?" Mary repeated with a tone someone might use to say, *They don't want to breathe?*

"Our Squirrel Resources department leads all sorts of training sessions. We even make them mandatory. But hardly anyone ever shows up," said Sam.

"Why do you think that might be?" asked Robin.

Sam thought about it: *Had he and his leadership team explained the purpose of the company or the employees' roles well enough that employees could understand which skills could help them achieve their purpose? Had they given employees the context for why those training sessions mattered or who the sessions would benefit? Had they ever asked their staff what stood in the way of their learning?* Sam knew the answers were no, no, and no.

"I suppose we haven't implemented the other principles of the power-with way," said Sam.

"Good point," said Adam. "When we have a sense of purpose, context, choice, and a safe space to fumble a bit while we're still new at something, learning tends to come naturally."

"Or *nut*-urally," Mary added (somewhat unnecessarily).

Sam thought about how his pups, Remi and Josie, nearly toppled over with excitement every time they learned something new.

They didn't need rewards or punishments. And neither did all those strange professor-student hybrids he met earlier at the university on the prairie. Sam realized with a start that even he had spent the morning relishing the experience of learning. Could it be that wanting to learn was natural after all?

"Fine," said Sam. "Maybe you have a point, but I still refuse to believe that just because most of us *want* to learn that we *can* learn anything we want."

"Most of us *can* learn," said Adam, "but that doesn't mean everyone *should* learn to get better at everything."

"That's true," said Mary with a giggle. "I bet it would take me twice as long as it would take any of you all to learn to juggle. I've had two left paws since I was a pup. It makes sense for most of us to do work that comes easily to us because it builds on our strengths."

"Right," said Adam. "The idea isn't to stick anyone into any role. The third principle simply reminds us that we build our power when we put more energy into cultivating infinite capability rather than collecting it from a finite pool."

"And how do you do that?" Sam asked.

Again, Adam looked to the stage. This time, Carol the groundhog held a thick stack of colorful leaves. She shuffled the deck, held it up to the group, and closed her eyes. A prairie dog closest to her selected one leaf and showed it to the others, who all nodded solemnly. He added it back to the deck, and Carol shuffled it so rapidly, the leaves transformed into a streak of color between her paws. With great flourish, she withdrew a leaf from the middle of the deck and held it up to the prairie dog. Applause and murmurs spread through the group.

"See that?" said Adam. "It looks impossible—like she has actual magical powers, right?"

Sam nodded. He had no idea how she had pulled that off.

"Well, pretty soon, most squirrels on her team will be able to do that trick as well as she does, and maybe even better," continued Adam.

"But how?" Sam said, thinking if she could pass on that skill, it would be an even more impressive magic trick.

"She applies the third principle to grow personal and collective power," said Adam. "Instead of spending all her time trying to track down the most talented squirrels, Carol pours that energy into teaching her team the skills they need, including working well alone and together. Then the troop helps each other keep learning and keep playing to individual strengths."

"The third principle also reminds us to distribute our power well," said Robin.

"But how?" Sam asked.

"At my company, we accidentally limited power distribution for a long time by creating unnecessary barriers to entry for our roles. We insisted on having two years of experience and the ability to burrow underground," she said.

"That seems reasonable," Sam protested, thinking of the long list of education and experience requirements for all of the jobs at his company.

"We thought so too," said Robin, "but then we decided to see what would happen if we removed some of our criteria. We discovered very quickly we were wrong about the qualifications that mattered most. We started looking for observable skills in our interviews rather than relying on impressive credentials. And we found ways to teach skills more quickly on the job and to build on individual strengths. Now our flying squirrels lead our search for areas in need of biodiversity. And our ground squirrels bury seeds deep enough to prevent them from freezing."[25]

Sam shook his head. He felt hope stir in his chest alongside a bone-deep exhaustion. Could building skills and preventing so-called barriers to entry really make a dent in his branch's talent shortage? Did Nuts for You even have enough time to find out? Condos grew faster than skills, didn't they? Besides, even if Sam did decide to implement these power-with principles in his workplace, wouldn't he just run into the same problems he had with his current strategy? What if the squirrels still refused to go his way?

CHECK-IN QUESTIONS: BE A CULTIVATOR, NOT A COLLECTOR

Let's take a closer look at how the third principle of the power-with way can work for you.

- *What skills or knowledge are missing on your team? Consider skills you need today and will need in the future, in addition to skill gaps that keep you from sharing your workload with others.*

- *How could you cultivate more of these skills on your team (e.g., clarify skills that matter most, provide learning time and resources, support job crafting and peer learning)?*

- *How might you reduce barriers to learning access (e.g., hire for skills vs. education or experience, improve onboarding, make growth opportunities accessible to more people)?*

"I believe you when you say these principles have worked for you," Sam said to the group, surprised to hear a quiver in his voice. "I want our squirrels to feel powerful and *be* powerful. I want our business and our whole community to have the power to overcome our obstacles. I want to lead together instead of leading all alone. But whoever built your community didn't have the problems I have. And they didn't have to convince everyone to change how they've done things all their lives and try something new." And then he tentatively added, "Did they?"

"Well, if you want to know the answer, you might as well just ask her," said Robin.

"Ask who?"

"The founder of our community."

Chapter 23

• • • • • • •

The Founder

"Finally!" cried Sam. "Will you bring me to meet your founder?"

"Um, Sam?" said Adam with a twinkle in his blue eyes. "You're standing right next to her."

Sam spun around to see who had snuck up behind him. Seeing no one, he turned again. He looked to his left and right, then back over at Adam with confusion all over his furry face. Finally, Sam looked at Mary, who held up her paw in a small wave.

"Wait," said Sam. "You? You're the founder?" Mary shrugged and smiled.

"I know it's hard to be-*leaf*."

Sam stared at her. Could it really be? Could this odd gray squirrel who'd been beside him all through this journey with her question-mark tail and her perpetual giggles really be the leader he'd been waiting to meet?

"But I asked you to take me to your leader," he said. "Why didn't you tell me it was you?"

"Because we don't have a single leader here," said Mary.

"Okay, fine," said Sam, "but you could have told me you own this place." He was surprised to feel anger and embarrassment bubbling up inside of him. He would have acted differently if he had known who she was. Wouldn't he?

"Sam," she said softly. "I may have been the one to start this community, but it does not belong to me."

"But you're in charge, aren't you?"

"I have responsibilities, if that's what you mean. My job is to help us fulfill our community's purpose to become a place of mutual flourishing."

"That's not what I mean, and you know it," said Sam. "You knew I was in trouble. You could have set up a trade with me, but you took me on an elaborate walking tour instead."

Sam felt that terrible falling sensation again like a branch had broken beneath him. He had let himself trust her. He had even begun to see her as a friend. But he realized now that she was a total stranger. He didn't know her or her intentions. And he had wasted so much precious time following her around and hoping it would lead to something.

Sam turned away and blinked back bitter tears. He scanned the room for an exit, and spotted a thick vine dangling from the sky-light. He muttered a goodbye to Robin and Adam, rushed over to the vine and, in a moment, he was back above ground.

The brightness of the day burned his eyes, and he squinted as he tried to make sense of his surroundings. Blinking, he looked up and saw he'd emerged under the sprawling oak tree at the edge of the prairie, where he'd first met the chipmunk professor. It was only hours ago, but it seemed like an entire season had passed. He looked for the professor's small, energetic figure, but no one was around. Sam felt like the only squirrel in the *squorld*. Now he'd have to figure out how to make it back to his part of the forest all on his own too. And even if he didn't get irreparably lost along the way, he'd come all the way home with empty paws.

Still, he had to get back. If nothing else, he owed it to his family to tell them what was going on, even if it made them lose all their faith in him. Sam looked all around, desperately trying to remember how he had wound up in this prairie. Then his gaze landed on a massive boulder jutting out from the ground, and a small but fully-stocked parcel of acorns at the foot of the rock. It was the very same bag he had dropped on his climb here that morning. A shock of greed surged through Sam's body. He scurried over to the satchel and swung it over his back. *Time to nut up or shut up*, he told himself.

But the steep climb up the boulder felt like an eternity. The rock face was equal parts slippery and jagged. So, Sam either scratched and scraped the pads of his paws or lost his grip and slid downward until he could catch himself again. Each time, he tightened his hold on the bag of acorns—the only thing he would have to show for his entire journey. By the time he reached the top of the rock, he was panting, and his whole body ached. Beneath him lay the log that was his shelter the night before, only now it looked like a twig in a green river of moss. And behind him . . .

Sam turned to look over the prairie one last time, only now he saw it with a stinging sadness tucked into his heart. Brilliant birds and butterflies still flitted between the trees. Squirrels of all colors and forms strolled together or gathered in circles to learn, work, or play. A whole family sat together, enjoying a meal. Free acorns still sprinkled the grass and glistened in the afternoon sun. Below the colorful tree tops lay the lab in the log and the bustling business district. And somewhere beneath the ground, there was the founder of this whole community, the squirrel who had raised Sam's hopes and dashed them. Why had he believed her when she said she'd help him? Why had he let himself get so distracted by her pointless principles of power when all that really mattered were the acorns he now clutched to his chest?

Sam glanced back over to the mossy side of the boulder and sighed, dreading the rough commute. But, as it turned out, he wouldn't have to make the climb down at all. A sharp shriek pierced the air, and a hawk swooped in and grasped Sam's shoulders.

Chapter 24

. . . .

Getting Help

The hawk's sharp claws dug into Sam's skin. Above him, giant wings stretched out and sliced through the air. Sam felt his feet leave the boulder. Helpless to do anything about it, he watched his acorns fly in all directions. And then he looked down in horror as the ground swelled before him. He screamed and thrashed, but the hawk's grip only tightened. And then Sam's scream grew louder and shaped into an unfamiliar word:

"Help!" he shouted. "Help!"

His voice rang out for just an instant, then vanished inside the hawk's ear-splitting cry. Something heavy whistled past them. Sam shut his eyes. Cold air rushed into his lungs. All around him, heavy wings beat furiously against the air. The ground slammed into Sam's body. And then the hawk's claws opened. Before the bird could grab him again, Sam scrambled to his feet and slipped into a hollow in a nearby log. A rock fell right before him, and then another, and another, until the hawk let out an angry scream and shot back up into the sky.

Sam lay for a long time in the silence that followed. He gripped a pile of leaves that lined the log and tried to quiet his breath.

His heart beat so wildly it seemed to echo through the entire tree trunk. He looked around to make sure he was alone. And only then did he recognize where he was. It was the hollow he'd slept in. It was the place he had woken up, holding the full bag of acorns that now lay empty beside him like a broken promise. *Some hero he turned out to be*, thought Sam. He had found a land full of acorns, but he didn't have a way to bring back even the smallest bundle, let alone live up to his vow to save his forest. Sam considered spending the rest of his life all alone in this log. And then he groaned because he realized he wasn't alone after all. Two small, gray feet stood at the opening of his hiding place.

"Sam," came the familiar voice. He knew right away it was Mary, but he didn't want to move. He didn't want to face her, to see her laughing at him again or hear her make some ridiculous pun about him giving her the silent *tree*-tment. And then he heard her say, "I'm so sorry, Sam." And, despite himself, he slid down from the hollow.

She looked smaller and older standing there before him. Her tail hung low. And there was no laughter in her dark eyes.

"Did you scare away that hawk?" he asked, already knowing the answer. She nodded and kicked at one of the rocks lying on the mossy ground. He had needed the help, of course. His life had depended on it. But Sam wished she hadn't been the one to help him. He had already felt small before her, and now he felt even smaller.

"I know I should be grateful," he said. "And I am. But I can't help wondering how it is that you're an expert in sharing power, and I'm left feeling so powerless."

It was (almost definitely) the most vulnerable thing he had ever said. And as soon as Sam heard those words leave his mouth, he wished he could take them back. But it was too late. He expected she would get angry or laugh or walk away, but she just took a deep breath and sat down on one of the rocks she had thrown.

"Because I screwed up, Sam," she said. "I didn't tell you about my role in the community even though I knew you'd want to know. I thought it would be a distraction. I thought I could help you more by sharing what we've learned here than by focusing on our acorns. But it was your right to decide how we'd spend our time together once you had all the information. I violated that right, and I misused my power."

"It's . . . it's okay," Sam mumbled. As usual, Mary had managed to surprise him. Sam was so unaccustomed to hearing a heartfelt apology, he didn't quite know what to do with it.

"I really don't control our community's resources, Sam," she continued, "but I meant it when I told you I wanted to help. So, if you still want to set up some kind of trade agreement, I'll do my best to try to introduce you to the right squirrels. If you just want to leave, I can help you find your way home. Or if there's any other way I can help you, just say the word."

Sam looked up into the sky and sighed. His anger left him, and he felt tired and empty. For the first time, he let himself face the truth: Even if she had the authority to set up a trade, there was nothing his company or his entire forest had to offer. Her community already had everything it needed. So, could it be that she hadn't let him down after all? Could it be that she had really been helping him in the best way she knew how? And was it possible that accepting her help now was the last chance Sam had? He took a step back and lowered himself onto a rock beside Mary.

"I think there is a way you can help me," he said. "Would you tell me how your community got started?"

Chapter 25

· · · · · · ·

Mutual Flourishing: Mary's Story

The night that fire tore through our forest, everyone scattered in all directions, grabbing any food we could carry and running for our lives. The roar of the flames was so loud, and the smoke was so thick. I couldn't take a breath for days after without feeling like my lungs were burning. We were all so dazed. So afraid.

"Stay smart and keep your distance from strangers," warned our elders.

So, at first, we tried to stick to the squirrels we knew, stay out of the others' way, and search for new places to live. But the fire did so much damage, and winter was snapping at our heels. So, three different groups of squirrels settled in the same part of the forest. We started off as strangers, but as the winter grew colder and the food supply scarcer, we turned against each other.

"Look out for yourself and your own" became the widespread advice.

We weren't selfish—at least that's not how we saw ourselves— but we only thought about our families and the squirrels we knew best. Everyone else was a threat and eventually a rival.

Every time we saw each other, we'd fight over scraps. It became such a force of habit that we continued to fight even when there was no more food left for any of us. I'm ashamed to admit it, but I hated those other squirrels. And I'm pretty sure I would have died hating them if it wasn't for a young pup who taught me a better way.

I was still foraging at dusk because I hadn't found enough food during the day. I knew the risks, but my stomach was growling. I was completely lost in thought when a child's shriek tore through the air above me.

"Watch out!" he cried. I looked up just in time to see an owl stretch her talons to grab me, and I darted out of the way. That pup risked his life to save mine, and he was part of the rival faction.

Once my paws stopped shaking, I climbed up his tree to thank him and his parents.

"Why did you help me?" I asked the pup.

"Because you needed help," he said simply.

It was the first time I had an actual conversation with someone from their group. I saw they were skinny and scared, just like us. They had hopes and dreams and disappointments, just like us.

That night I went to sleep with an empty stomach but a very full heart. And the next day, and the days after that, I foraged non-stop so I could share my food with all the squirrels and many of the other animals too. The squirrels in my group were upset about it at first.

"You're picking some stranger over us," my neighbor scolded when she spotted me bringing food to someone from a competing group. Even the squirrels I tried to help questioned my intentions.

But I kept sharing my food whenever I had a bit to spare, and I stopped to talk to any squirrel who crossed my path.

Little by little, more of us began to do the same. We started looking out for each other, and we began to feel safer together. Eventually, I invited the three groups to join together as one community with one shared purpose: to become a place of mutual flourishing.

"Tell us your vision for this community," said a skeptical squirrel from my group.

"That's all I've got so far," I admitted. "I believe we can build the kind of community that makes each and every one of us stronger. But I need your help figuring out how to do it."

"If this is going to work, we'll have to stay on the move," said another squirrel.

"That's too dangerous," said a member of the other group. "We need a safe place to call home. Somewhere better than here."

"Too risky," argued a young squirrel from the third group. "Who knows what's out there and if it's worse than what we have now? We should stay here."

I could tell a s-quarrel was coming, so I hopped up on a stump and started applauding. Everyone stopped arguing and looked at me like I had two tails.

"Can you see how much we're already benefiting from having so many different perspectives?" I said. "Now we just have to integrate them. Can anyone think of a way to balance our needs for stability, safety, and opportunity?"

There was a very long, very uncomfortable silence, but then someone said, "Well, how about if most of us stay here until springtime, and, in the meantime, we gather a group of explorers to look for other locations?"

Another silence followed, but a few heads began to nod. Several other squirrels proposed ideas, and more voices chimed in to build on them. They began to move together into one big circle, and from my spot on the stump, I could no longer tell which group was which. It was at that moment I knew there was hope for our community.

Chapter 26

· · · · · · · ·

Principle #4: Build a Community, Not a Crowd

"That's a really nice story," said Sam, feeling genuinely moved and also a little disappointed because he couldn't see a way for it to help his situation. "But I guess it doesn't apply to business."

"Oh, but it does!" said Mary, hopping up from the rock as though it had suddenly gotten hot. "It's not just some *sappy* story. It actually gets right to the heart of the fourth principle of the power-with way. It's a principle that applies to just about every aspect of how we work, learn, and live together."

"Okay, what is it?" asked Sam. "What's the fourth principle?"

"*Build a community, not a crowd*," said Mary.

"Community?" Sam repeated. "What exactly is a community?"

"A community is a group that relies on each other to achieve its purpose," said Mary.

"But that's the first principle," said Sam. "Follow a purpose, not a person."

"Well, having a shared purpose is an important part of being in a community, but it's not enough," said Mary. "An audience can come together with the shared purpose of watching a magic show. But that doesn't make it a community, does it?"

"No," said Sam. "I guess not."

"Why do you think that is?"

"I guess because the audience members are independent. They can be a crowd of strangers, and it would have little impact on their experience. And they can come and go, but the show would stay more or less the same."

"Exactly!" said Mary. "A crowd is independent. A community is *interdependent*."

"Okay, in that case every company is a community," said Sam. "Bosses rely on their workers. Workers rely on their employers. Employees rely on each other. Why even call it one of the principles?"

"You're right," said Mary. "Any time we work together, some kind of community emerges. The problem is most of us don't think about it that way, so we don't build our communities deliberately. In the end, we're left feeling like a crowd—sometimes even a mob." A shadow seemed to pass over her face and Sam recognized the expression.

"Like the squirrels in your forest after the fire," he said softly, and she nodded. "I guess I'm still kind of stumped about them. They hated each other," he went on, thinking of his own feelings toward squirrels in neighboring parts of his forest. "How did you convince them to go your way?"

"I didn't," said Mary. "I asked them to cocreate the way. Anyone who decided to join had a role and a voice in how we did things. It was their community just as much as it was mine. I thought I'd have to talk them into it. But it turns out what matters more than getting buy-in is getting build-in.[26] Most of us only feel a part of something when we're building it. That's the most important tenet of community: it's cocreated."

"I guess I can see that being the case with a startup," Sam said, "but you can't cocreate a company like ours. It was already built generations ago."

"I think when it comes to community, there's no such thing as already being built," said Mary, "only the continuous process of building. Community is really more of a verb than a noun."

Sam got up from his rock and started pacing back and forth across the soft, mossy ground. He rubbed his temples. That overwhelming pressure of wonder and frustration was building up in his head again. He could imagine—albeit without a great deal of clarity—implementing the other power-with principles. He could picture himself articulating a clear purpose for his branch. He could see himself relying on context instead of control. He could cultivate his staff's skills. But how could he possibly let them cocreate a company that didn't even belong to him?

"But how?" he asked. "How can I cocreate community with my staff?"

"That's something you'll have to ask them," said Mary. "It's the whole *co* part. But one good way to start is to invite input on your goals and strategy."

"But wouldn't that just slow us all down?" said Sam. "I have a hard enough time getting just two squirrels on my management team to agree with each other. I can't imagine how long it would take to reach consensus across the whole branch."

"True," said Mary. "It's why we rarely aim for consensus. We generally have lots of decision-makers, and they each make decisions in their domains. If it impacts others, they get input first. They might not use it all, but they integrate as many perspectives as they can."

"Sounds like a lot of extra work," said Sam.

"Oh, it can be a *pine* in the neck," Mary admitted. "But it's almost always worth it in the end. It makes our decisions better and our execution faster."

"But how do you decide on your decision-makers?"

"Usually, the decision-maker is the person closest to the situation with the most relevant role," said Mary. "But that doesn't mean the decision-maker has to come up with all the ideas."

"What do you mean?"

"When you operate like a community, ideas can come from anywhere!" said Mary. "It's one of the most exciting things about a power-with way of working. Most of our businesses invite their team members to propose new initiatives. They also ask cross-functional task forces to come up with all kinds of organizational solutions."

"How about when it comes to distributing power?" asked Sam a little nervously. "Does the fourth principle help you do that too?"

"Oh yes!" said Mary. "The fourth principle helps us prevent decision-making power from getting too concentrated in high-stakes situations. So, for example, most of our companies use at least two decision-makers and a tie-breaker when they hire, promote, or fire an employee. It makes their decisions better, and it helps keep bias out too. We also rotate many of our leadership roles so power doesn't get stuck with one person for too long."

"You're saying I'd have to give up my own power for this to work?"

"You can do as little or as much as you'd like, Sam," said Mary. "These are principles, not rules. You can make a lot of changes or just a few small ones. You can use all the principles or just one. You'll still see the benefit, as long as you remember the most important part."

"The most important part?"

"That the surest way to grow power is to share it."

CHECK-IN QUESTIONS: BUILD A COMMUNITY, NOT A CROWD

Check in with yourself about the fourth principle of the power-with way:

- *What's an example of something you built alone that you could have cocreated together with your team (e.g., goals, strategy, policies, systems, events)?*

- *How might you make your team feel more like a community by leading together (e.g., ask for input, integrate perspectives, invite proposals and task forces, create shared rituals)?*

- *What are some ways you could reduce decision-making power concentration (e.g., distribute decision-making authority across different roles, have two decision-makers and a tie-breaker for high-stakes decisions, rotate formal authority)?*

"I don't know," Sam sighed. "Even if what you're telling me is true, I don't have much left that's even worth sharing. I marched into the forest yesterday determined to inspire my company. And I'm going to crawl out of it today with nothing to show for all my efforts."

"Well, this could be a start," said Mary. And she plopped back down on the rock beside him, holding open the satchel Sam had assumed was empty. All the way down on the bottom lay one very small, yet perfectly plump acorn.

Okay, here we go. Sam's journey home is about to begin. He may only have one acorn left, but he's also bringing back all four principles of the power-with way:

1. **Follow a purpose, not a person:** When a who looms larger than the why, learning and decision-making suffer and progress slows as people wait for orders. When purpose is clear, people feel a greater sense of meaning while making faster progress toward their shared goals.

2. **Rely on context, not control:** Too much control harms motivation and creativity while increasing stress, and a lack of context limits decision-making quality. When you make context accessible and clear, it helps people take action more independently, thoughtfully, and joyfully.

3. **Be a cultivator, not a collector:** Attempting to collect people from a small, finite crop of talent (rather than cultivating an infinite field) limits organizational capability, diversity, and agility. Instead, invest in building technical, intrapersonal, and interpersonal skills on your team, and reduce your barriers to growth and learning.

4. **Build a community, not a crowd:** Feeling like an impersonal crowd (rather than an interconnected community) causes disengagement and inefficiencies. Instead, invite input, participation, and collaboration in company decisions, and distribute decision-making.

Each principle relies on a deliberate balance of power: (1) increase (informal and formal) personal power and (2) distribute it well. At the end of this book, you'll find a bank of ideas, but for now, check in with yourself:

- Which principle resonates with you?

- Which principle feels most foreign or uncomfortable?

- Which principle will help you become the leader you want to be and address the problems or challenges you face? (Hint: think back to your answers in Part I of this book.)

- What is a small experiment you can run to see the principle in action?

Speaking of taking action, any minute now, Sam will find the courage to use his new power-with ideas to lead together. Notice what he does well and not so well. Notice how he's changed since you first met him. And most important, notice how your own thinking is changing.

PART IV

PRINCIPLES IN ACTION

Chapter 27

• • • • • • •

Coming Home

With Mary's help, Sam made it back to the part of the forest he recognized from the day before. A cold mist began to rise up from the ground, but the setting sun cast a warm, golden beam all the way down his path home. He turned to Mary to say something, only he couldn't figure out what to say. He wanted to thank her. He wanted to tell her he was sorry. He wanted to ask her what his first step should be once he got back to work. But instead, he just smiled, and she smiled back. Without another word, she turned around and disappeared into the dusk.

"*Cedar* later," Sam whispered.

For a moment, he could see the bright white tip of her question-mark tail, and then she was gone. Sam just stood there for a little while, holding his single acorn. Then, he lifted his tail high and faced the road ahead. He had some options before him.

One path led to his branch, where he was pretty sure his workers were barely working and his management team barely managing. The other path led to his boss's office, where he was pretty sure

Mr. Walnuts was deciding whether he should fire him or throw another rock directly at his head. The last path led back to Amara and the kids who, he was pretty sure, either hated him by now or had decided they were better off without him. Each path terrified him, so Sam took a deep breath and chose to take the path that scared him most.

The sky was smeared dark pink and purple by the time he got there. His paws shook as he climbed up the tree. The pine scent of his house reached him before he was even halfway up, and it smelled like home. For once, Sam didn't rehearse what he would say. He didn't anticipate Amara's words. He just wanted to see his family.

But even before he entered his house, he could tell it was empty. The walls only held quiet. The nest was cold. Were the pups at the clinic with Amara? Or did they all move out to live with Amara's sister? He placed his single acorn in the corner and crawled back out, determined to find out. But just then, he heard the sweetest of sounds.

"Dad?" Josie called from far below.

"Sam?" came Amara's voice.

"Dad! Dad!" cried Remi.

Within seconds, Sam was on the ground beside them, wrapping his family up in his arms and tail. He shut his eyes and breathed in the sweet, oaky scent of their fur, and nothing else on this earth mattered. They stood like that together for a long time, then Josie pulled away.

"Why are you crying, Dad?" she asked, looking up at his face intently.

"I'm just so happy to be with you all," said Sam, not even trying to wipe away his tears. Then, looking at Amara, he said, "And I'm sorry I was away—not just last night but all the times I haven't been here for you." Amara looked into his eyes, and the tip of her tail trembled.

"Where were you, Dad?" asked Remi.

"I got lost," said Sam, "but a strange squirrel from another part of the forest helped me. She gave me shelter but, even more important, she taught me how to be a better leader and, I hope, a better member of this family too." Amara's eyes widened. Then that wry smirk Sam loved so much spread across her face.

"We'll be the judge of that," she said. "But for now, we're just happy to have you back exactly as you were." And then she kissed him and hopped up the tree to their house. The pups followed, giggling over nothing in particular. Sam watched their tiny orange tails for a little while, his heart squeezing inside his chest. And then he followed too.

They tucked in Josie and Remi and sang them lullabies together. In no time, the pups were fast asleep. Sam looked up from their small, furry faces to see that Amara was watching him.

"I have a lot to tell you, Am," he whispered.

She nodded.

They slipped back out into the chilly evening air and sat side by side, pressing into one another for warmth and for the sweet relief of each other's touch. And he told her everything. About the condo development. About the forest recession. About his attempt to gather acorns that wound up getting him dangerously lost. About his close call with the hawk. About Mary and her strange community and their four principles of leading together. About his realization that Amara was the best leader he knew.

For the first time since they met, he named his mistakes and admitted he didn't have all the answers. Amara nodded and looked off into the distance as he spoke. When he was finished, they sat in silence together for a while, and then she said, "I can see how these principles apply to our family too." Sam twisted on the branch to face her, and she went on. "Follow a purpose not a person—we've been so busy debating over our individual career needs, we lost sight of what's best for the well-being of our family. Creating a safe, loving home together is our shared purpose, isn't it?"

"Yes," said Sam, amazed that it seemed to take her seconds to make sense of what had taken him so long to wrap his mind around. "That's right. And I guess the stronger our family is, the stronger each of us will be too."

"And we haven't given one another enough context either, have we?" she said. "We've just attempted to control each other through criticism or praise." Then, seeing his surprise, she added, "Yes, yes, I said *we*. I'm just as much to blame for it as you are. Well, almost as much." They pressed into each other more firmly and laughed. "We could try being a little more open about our needs and our feelings with each other," she said. "We can explain why we're asking for something instead of just demanding it."

"I'd like that very much," he said. "But how about the third principle: be a cultivator, not a collector?"

"I think that one applies too," she said. "We've treated each other as though we can't change. But squirrel teeth never stop growing, so neither should we, right?"

"That's right," said Sam. "I guess I never thought about how important it is to learn to be a family together. But it's a skill we can build like any other."

"And the last one—what was it?" she said, "build a community, not a crowd? Haven't we felt like strangers living under one roof lately?" Sam nodded, the tears returning to his eyes. He had been so distracted by his own loneliness he hadn't noticed she'd been feeling it too. "Maybe it's time we work together, become stronger together," she said. "We'll need that strength for whatever comes next."

"Yes," said Sam. "Yes, we will."

He still felt scared and overwhelmed and not yet ready to face whatever was waiting for him ahead. But now he knew he wouldn't have to face it alone.

CHECK-IN QUESTIONS: EVERYDAY POWER

Sam is learning how power shows up in each of his relationships. How about you?

- *Aside from the workplace, where else might you benefit from a power-with approach?*

- *Which of the power-with principles would you like to apply?*

Chapter 28

. . . .

Back at the Office

Sam started his morning at the branch by calling another all-paws meeting. His management team and his entire staff filed in without question, objection, or apparent interest. It had only been two days since Sam last saw them, but as he watched their lackluster arrival, he was struck by how beaten down they looked. How had he never noticed the drag in their step? The distrust in their eyes? The tense silence that spread through any room he entered? Had he really been so drunk on power that he hadn't paid attention to anyone but himself?

He really took them in now as they stood before him, waiting for the meeting to start (or, more likely, to be over). Each of them was an individual with ideas, needs, goals, personal lives, and stories. Each of them had the ability to be powerful, to make one another powerful. But how? Sam clutched the small, shiny acorn Mary gave him and tried to ignore that his paws were shaking.

"You may be wondering why I wasn't at the office yesterday," he started. Then reading the looks on their faces, he said: "Or . . . you had no idea I wasn't at the office and were just relieved you hadn't run into me." A murmur swept through the audience, along with a few surprised giggles.

Something in their expressions shifted ever so slightly, and it gave Sam the courage to go on: "The truth is I headed into the forest alone, thinking I could outgather everyone here. I planned to come back with so many acorns that I would show you all the way forward, and our path to success would be undeniable. And then I figured I'd use every threat and reward I could think up to make you go my way. I thought that's what it meant to be a great leader.

"Well, as you all probably could have told me if I'd asked, there were no acorns to be found. I got lost, in more ways than one. But getting lost led me to a community far from our forest that is overflowing with acorns." Another murmur floated through the crowd.

"Were you able to bring them back?" asked a familiar voice. Sam looked out to see Paloma, the squirrel who had unintentionally taught him about the importance of informal power. And for the first time since he had met her, he looked into her bright, brown eyes and smiled.

"I brought back one," he said, holding out the small acorn again for everyone to see. The murmur from the group grew louder. "I tried to set up a trade agreement, but the community had no need for it. I know this acorn doesn't look like much, but it represents something much bigger—bigger even than an entire tree trunk–full of acorns.

"You see, acorns are power among us squirrels, aren't they? This community I wandered into could have kept their power all to themselves. But instead, they shared it with me. And they helped me realize I have to share my own power too." No one said anything in reply, not even Paloma. So, Sam added, "Basically, they helped me see that I've been a real son of a *birch* to you all, and I have to learn to be a better leader."

There was another stretch of silence, and then Paloma said, "Well, it's about time!"

And everyone burst into laughter, including Sam. After that, something seemed to open up in the group. Their posture became more relaxed, their eyes brighter.

"How about I start by sharing the power of information?" Sam offered. "If you can trust me with your questions, I promise you I'll trust you with the answers."

They were tentative at first, but the questions began to trickle in and then flow more quickly. Someone asked about the condo-development rumor, and Sam confirmed it was true. Fear surged through the group, but it was entwined with relief to have the information out in the open. Nobody freaked out. Nobody left the meeting. Sam asked his management team to share what they knew about it, and they did so with clarity and care. Even Ravi, the squirrel resources manager, rose to the challenge. Then, someone else asked what they planned to do about the forest recession, and his entire management team shot Sam a collective look of panic.

"Well, to be honest with you, I don't know," said Sam, and the panic on his management team's faces intensified. "And the reason I don't know is that I've been trying to use my personal power to solve this problem all on my own. But it's too big for me. What we need to do now is grow our collective power, so we can come up with the solution. We need to lead together. So, I can't tell you yet how we'll figure this out. But I can tell you there is no doubt in my mind that we *will* figure it out together."

Another squirrel asked about the community Sam visited. So, he told them all about the university, the lab in the log, the business district, the four principles of the power-with way, and the strange squirrel with the question-mark tail who saved his life twice and gave him the knowledge that just might save their branch.

"If you're willing to give it a go," said Sam, "I think we can all benefit from trying the power-with way. I believe Nuts for You and our entire forest will be stronger if we lead this company together." Sam saw heads nodding and tails swishing with nervous excitement. Many in the group turned to look at Paloma, but her expression was inscrutable.

"What does it mean to try the power-with way?" she asked. Everyone looked back to Sam.

"Uh," Sam started. Suddenly, the little acorn in his grip felt moist. It took Sam a second to understand his paws were sweating. "I guess I don't really know that either," he admitted.

Chapter 29

· · · · · · ·

Resistance

Sam climbed back to his office, thinking the all-paws meeting went better than expected, despite its lackluster ending. Everyone handled the condo news well. And he hadn't (yet) caused a panic with his admission that he didn't have all the answers. Sure, Jack Walnuts might fire him on the spot if he found out. And yes, it was a violation of everything he had tried to achieve with his leadership in the past. *Treeson,* Mary would call it. But that was the point, wasn't it? Sharing power meant sharing the responsibility of finding solutions together. Sam was beginning to feel cautiously optimistic, but then he saw his management team standing outside his office, glaring at him.

"Are we still part of the leadership team or not?" Francesca, the finance manager, blurted out as soon as she saw him.

"Of course you are," said Sam, taking a couple of steps back.

"Well, then," she said, crossing her glossy gray arms, "do you think it would have been nice to give us a little advance notice before making that kind of presentation to the entire branch?"

"Oh," said Sam. "Oh, yes. You're right. I'm so sorry, everyone."

The apology seemed to knock Francesca a bit off balance, so Mila, the marketing manager, hopped in: "Sam, we're about to face the most severe forest recession in generations," she said in a pleading tone. "We need a business strategy, not a philosophy."

"Especially not one cooked up by a bunch of hippie squirrels," Francesca added, having regained her composure.

"Yeah," said Ravi, furiously scratching a bald patch on his arm, "and we don't even have time to meet our quotas, let alone do a whole company restructuring. It's something Squirrel Resources could have told you if you had just checked with us."

"And I don't know if you've noticed," added Mila, "but everyone around here is already exhausted. I can't see how giving them 'company cocreation' responsibilities on top of their existing workload can make anything any better."

"Even if they had the time it wouldn't matter," said Francesca. "They gather and sell nuts. They don't have the skills to lead a company."

"Some of them don't even have the skills to gather and sell nuts," added Ravi.

Sam's head began to spin. He had expected that trying the power-with way would be challenging, but he didn't expect to meet so much resistance so quickly, especially from his management team. In his rush to share his own power, he assumed they'd be eager to share theirs. But, of course, it made sense they weren't excited about the sudden change. He had spent a long time thinking about the power-with principles. They were just hearing about them for the first time. But what could he do about it?[27]

A small, gruff voice in the back of his head (that sounded an awful lot like Jack Walnuts) told him it was time to show them the way and make them go his way. But that couldn't be the path to the power-with way, could it? Did it make sense to use a power-over strategy to create a power-with result? And then Sam heard another voice in his head, this one sounding like Mary. *What matters more than getting buy-in is getting build-in*, said this bright voice. And then another voice, sounding a lot like a chipmunk professor he knew, added, *I can tell you what I think, but what really matters is what* you *think.*

So, Sam swallowed his urge to debate with them or attempt to convince them, and he asked them questions instead. "I'd like to check if we're all trying to achieve the same thing," said Sam (thinking of the first principle). "Do you all see figuring out how to save our branch as our shared purpose?"

"Well, yes," said Francesca. "I suppose that's our ultimate goal."

"Okay, and just so we all have shared context," Sam continued (leaning on the second principle), "how likely do you think we are to achieve our purpose if we keep doing things the same way we have been?"

"Not very likely at all," said Mila, and the others nodded, albeit begrudgingly.

"I think so too," said Sam. "So, it sounds like we have a shared purpose, and we agree something needs to change if we want to reach it, but you're not sure if the changes I'm proposing are the right way to go." His management team nodded again, looking ever so slightly less resistant. "Could you share what concerns you most about giving the power-with principles a try?"

"Well, for starters we don't have the skills," said Ravi. "We don't know what we're doing."

"Yet," said Sam (remembering the third principle). "But I bet we could figure it out together, especially if we take the time to learn from each other."

"We don't have time," snapped Francesca.

"Or energy," whined Mila.

"That's true," said Sam. "Those are all fair points." His blood pressure began to buzz in his ears. He had no idea what he should do now. But then he thought back to Mary's story and the fourth principle. "So . . . I wonder if we could come up with a plan together that's quick and easy to implement and doesn't rely on any of us being experts? We can be like the lab in the log, testing out new ideas to see what works. If we don't like something, we can scrap it and try something else."

Mila clasped her tail in her paws. Francesca rolled her eyes. And Ravi scratched one of the shiny new bald patches on his shoulder. They were silent for a long time, until Francesca finally let out a huff and said, "Okay, fine. Let's see what we can come up with."

They talked and talked. Gradually, their voices softened and their arms uncrossed. Eventually, Francesca suggested they apply the first power-with principle to align all their staff around a single shared purpose: to save the branch. She announced she was willing to try new things as long as she didn't have to give up any of the hard-earned perks that came with her role. Her title would stay untouched. Her office would remain as large and private as ever.

It was fascinating, thought Sam. Unlike the classic *power-grabber* style of Mr. Walnuts, Francesca was a vocal advocate for empowering employees. She preached the importance of asking for input, giving options, and delegating work. But Sam saw now that when she said "empower," she didn't mean "give power." Her leadership approach was just about as power-over-oriented as Sam's had been. She did ask for input, but she rarely used it. She offered her staff options, but only the ones she approved of. She delegated often, but only minor tasks she didn't want to do herself. She said collaborative-sounding things like "let's get the team onboard" and "be customer-centric," but it was really just code for "let's get them to do what we want" and "the ends justify the means."

Her team members seemed to respect her, but they were also intimidated by her, and they relied on her completely. If Francesca was out of the office, either their work stood still or they scurried aimlessly in all directions. She behaved like a *power masker*—an empowerment imposter. *Empowster*, Sam thought and chuckled to himself, thinking Mary would approve.

Mila said she very much supported the second principle of relying on context instead of control and had never liked the idea of controlling her team in the first place. She proposed giving everyone the option to work any hours they wanted, so long as they were present for meetings. Francesca winced at the suggestion but agreed to give it a try. Mila also committed to loosen her sales policies so her team could experiment. But when Francesca offered to lead a daily huddle for the whole branch so everyone received the same information at the same time, Mila's eyes bulged.

"But it will be so stressful for them," she said, wringing her tail in her paws.

"If they think everything's going fine then suddenly lose their jobs, won't that be a whole lot more stressful?" Francesca retorted.

Mila took in a big, shaky breath and agreed. But she couldn't bring herself to give her team feedback on any work they weren't doing well. She admitted feedback would provide helpful context, but she was sure it would hurt their feelings too much.

"I'll tell them eventually," she promised, "but everyone is under too much pressure right now. It's just not a good time to put more on their shoulders."

Sam remembered hearing her use these exact words in the past. He considered her leadership style. While Mr. Walnuts has a power-grabber style and Francesca took a power-masker approach, Mila led more like a *power sapper*. She didn't use a power-over approach because she was power-hungry but because she wanted to shield her team. Deep down, she believed they were fragile, and she didn't want to break them. But, Sam now understood, the less power she gave them, the weaker they became. It was unintentional, but the impact was undeniable. Mila's entire department was constantly anxious and overwhelmed.

When they got to the third principle, Ravi pointed out he'd always believed in cultivating talent in-house instead of just collecting it externally. But it was hard to get any practical suggestions from him about power-with experiments they could try.

"Isn't this your area of expertise?" Francesca said with unveiled disdain.

"Yes, but it's complicated," said Ravi. "And complex. And harder than it sounds."

As Sam listened to this exchange, he realized that if Mr. Walnuts acted like a power grabber, Francesca a power masker, and Mila a power sapper, then Ravi's style must be a *power shrugger*. He rarely took initiative and waited for orders to come from somewhere above him. He had a power-under approach and seemed to both resent it and require it. The result was less power for him and for everyone around him, except the individuals telling him what to do. It was no wonder his whole department seemed to be as defeated as he was.

Sam was tempted to fall into his well-worn habit of telling Ravi what to do, but then he remembered observing the conversations at Alfie's university where everyone spent as much time listening as they did talking. Wasn't conversational turn-taking the most basic act of sharing power?[28] Wasn't it a way to cultivate the strength of the whole group instead of just collecting ideas from the loudest voices in the room? So, Sam decided to try something new.

"Ravi," he said, "I bet you do have great ideas to share, but I get the feeling we're all rushing you and putting too much pressure on you to solve it on your own. How about we each take five minutes to think it over, then go around and share our proposals?"

Ravi blinked twice, then three times. It was a suggestion and a tone he had never heard from Sam before. Francesca rolled her eyes again, but Mila clasped her paws together in delight. Sam watched doubt, fear, and then suspicion float by like clouds across Ravi's face, but Ravi nodded, and they all began to think. When five minutes passed, Ravi's face wore a new expression.

"Okay if I go first?" he said.

"Please do!" said Mila.

"Well, since we don't have the time or resources to run a new Squirrel Resources program, I was thinking we could create cross-training opportunities between the different departments like the university you told us about. That way we're cultivating new knowledge, sharing more context, and starting to build a sense of community," said Ravi. For a moment, his eyes glowed with more energy than Sam had ever seen in him, but then he shrugged and looked away as though he said something embarrassing.

"Actually," said Francesca slowly, "actually, that's a pretty good idea, Ravi." Sam and Mila nodded, and Ravi looked up again with renewed zest.

By the time they got to the fourth power-with principle, their ideas flowed more quickly and creatively. They all agreed they wanted their branch to feel like more of a community than the crowd it felt like now. Francesca suggested holding office hours so any employee could come to them with questions and suggestions. Mila volunteered her office. And Ravi proposed they launch a cross-functional task force to come up with new ideas to save the branch.

Everyone spoke. Everyone listened. And Sam got the sense everyone left the conversation more hopeful than they had been in a long time. Now all they had to do was put their ideas into practice. Sam straightened his tail, pulled back his shoulders, and thought, *How hard could it be?*

CHECK-IN QUESTIONS: POWER PROFILE

Sam spotted several power profiles on his team. Can you think of people you know whose leadership approach falls into each category?

- **Power grabber** *(overtly power-over style—take control and give orders)*

- **Power masker** *(power-over style but masks it with empowering rhetoric)*

- **Power sapper** *(power-over style as a result of shielding others from responsibility)*

- **Power shrugger** *(power-under style—avoids making decisions and taking responsibility)*

- **Power-with** *(uses own power to grow shared power)*

Chapter 30

• • • • • • •

The Messy Middle

By the end of the month, Sam came to the conclusion that this change was going to be very hard.

At first, his staff was reluctant to say much of anything. Sam was tempted to write them off as either uninterested or incapable, or both, but then he remembered Erich, the shy ground squirrel from Mary's community. He had good ideas, but he admitted it was scary to speak up at first even when he knew he had the power to do so. He had to get used to that new level of power. And his community had to prove to him that using it was safe.[29] So, Sam persisted.

"What can we do better as a branch?" he asked. "What's something we haven't tried yet that might help us stay safe? What feedback do you have about our marketing strategy?"

Only silence followed at first, and he bit his tongue to keep from filling it with the sound of his own voice. But eventually, feedback began to roll in. At first, Sam's ego fought back inside his head, but he reminded himself that his job was to keep learning and to help his team feel safe speaking up.

"I see what you mean," he said when Paloma suggested they were too focused on gathering.

"How about storage?" she said. "I think the storage department might be feeling left out." Sam wanted so badly to argue or, at the very least, to defend his position. But instead, he said, "I really appreciate that you brought this up. I'll visit the storage team today to explore some ideas."

After that first conversation, Sam met with Paloma on a regular basis to get her guidance. She seemed to know everyone at the branch well, and anytime she joined one of their meetings, her presence was a shortcut to their trust. Little by little, these efforts began to pay off. When squirrels whose voices Sam never heard before spoke up, he felt a surge of exhilaration. But within a week, the exhilaration turned to panic.

It was as though he'd yanked open the acorn safe in his office, and all the nuts came tumbling out. Once his staff began talking, they couldn't seem to stop. Once they started to trust that they could really take the power they were offered, they seemed to grab it and run.

His management team's attempt to align with their staff around the branch's purpose resulted in so much debate that Sam felt dazed about what it was Nuts for You actually did. Their newly loosened sales policies caused conflict internally and confusion externally. And the squirrels who joined one of the many new task forces soon felt overworked and underappreciated.

Sam expected Mr. Walnuts to show up and take back control at any moment. Instead, he was met with an angry row of squirrels outside his office. Francesca, Mila, and Ravi all looked ready for a fight. Only this time, they couldn't use Sam's office to meet because he made it available to anyone at the branch to use for any reason they wanted.

"Do you know what they said to me when I told them we had an important meeting to take in here?" Francesca demanded as soon as she saw Sam. He opened his mouth to speak, but she continued, "That *they* also had an important meeting to take! Can you believe it?"

Sam felt a flutter in his stomach. Wasn't his staff's willingness to use his office a sign that their new approach was working? He was about to say as much to his management team. But then he glanced from the doorway to the furry fury that was Francesca's face and understood that he had to say something else: "You're right," said Sam. "We haven't really figured out how to share space yet. I'm thinking we can get better at giving context for why we need our meeting rooms and when we need them. How about we invite a small task force to figure out how to use our common spaces well?"

"I think we've had enough task forces around here lately, Sam," said Francesca, her anger mutating into unnerving calm. "Tell him, Mila," she said.

"Uh, well, Sam, I'm sorry," said Mila, "but this just isn't working. I like the idea of leading together. I do. But it's chaos out there. And I don't even know what my job as a leader is anymore."

Sam looked at their tense faces. He looked past them at the boisterous meeting happening inside his room. And then he sighed. It was a heavy sound that was more like two sighs in one. One was a sigh of deep disappointment. He believed in the power-with way now, and he wanted it to work. The other was a sigh of relief. He had tried, hadn't he? They had all done their best. Sure, their old way of doing things hadn't worked, but at least it was familiar. At least they'd all know how to do their jobs again, even if they didn't exactly know how to do them well. Sam looked up to see Francesca and Mila nodding in agreement, but Ravi was rubbing his shiny, bald head.

"What's on your mind, Ravi?" Sam asked.

"I'm thinking if we stop now, we'll be throwing out the bird with the birdbath," said Ravi. "I'm also frustrated. But not because I think we're giving away too much power but because I think we're not giving away enough."

"What?" Francesca nearly shouted, her disquieting calm dissipating.

"What do you mean, Ravi?" Sam asked.

"Well, the four of us decided how to give our staff more power," he said. "We picked the tactics, and they executed. We haven't actually asked them to weigh in on how we should share power. We're still going about this in a power-over kind of way."

"So, what exactly do you propose?" asked Francesca.

"What if we just take this challenge to the team?" said Ravi.

"You mean ask them how to make sharing power work instead of trying to solve it ourselves?" said Mila. Ravi nodded emphatically. "Hmm," Mila said after a moment, "I think I see your point."

"I think so, too," said Sam, a glint of hope finding its way back into his chest.

"What?" Francesca exclaimed again. "Have you all completely lost your nuts? Am I the only one around here who actually cares about saving the branch? Have you forgotten the condo construction is just months away?" Her question spilled a pained silence across the group.

"It's the first thing I think about when I open my eyes each morning," Sam said eventually.

"Me too," said Mila.

"Same here," said Ravi.

"Saving our branch is our shared purpose," Sam said quietly. "That's why I think it's important we try solutions we've never tried before to see if they can get us results we've never gotten before." Francesca groaned, but she uncrossed her arms, so Sam decided to chance it and continue: "I agree the way we're doing things now isn't working," he said. "Maybe it's because we're in the messy middle of change, or maybe it just won't work for us here. I don't know. But I think we owe it to ourselves, our team, and our forest to find out. Ravi brought up an idea I'd very much like to try: bring our power-sharing struggles to the team, and ask if they can think of solutions. Is there anything that might make you more open to trying it?"

Francesca said nothing for a while. The four of them just stood outside the room that used to be Sam's office and looked at each other. Short snatches of excited conversation flitted by them like sparks coming off a flame. Finally, Francesca sighed and ran a paw through her shiny fur.

"Fine," she said. "I'll get behind yet another experiment. But can we agree to give it only one more month? And if we're still behind on our metrics, then we'll throw out this bird and her bath?"

"Deal!" said Sam. And the others agreed.

CHECK-IN QUESTIONS:
PREPARE FOR CHANGE

Change rarely looks good when we're in the middle of it. Some frustration is inevitable. Still, it's worth pausing to consider what might go wrong with your own power-with experiment so your journey will be a little smoother. Jot down any bumps in the road you can anticipate. How might you avoid them or get through them well?

Chapter 31

· · · · · · ·

High Tails

Sam ducked under the nearly bare branches of the High Tails club willow tree, and his heartbeat quickened. Sylvio, Eva, Jose, and several other members of the business leader nut-work were already there. He reminded himself that he had nothing to worry about. Sure, his business was different from theirs now, and *he* was different too. But hadn't he learned by now that difference is a strength? Still, something in the atmosphere made all the squirrels puff up their chests and tails and, unknowingly, Sam did too. Only Jose's comment made him aware of it.

"Let me go out on a limb here and guess," said Jose. "You're having another great month at your branch."

"Me?" said Sam. "Oh, well, actually we are."

"At least *someone* here is," said Eva. "What's going on over there, anyway? We've been hearing all sorts of strange rumors."

"Sounds like you know the law, and you've been making them go your way," said Sylvio with his signature mix of envy and admiration.

Despite himself, Sam felt a surge of pride well up in his chest. He wanted to brag. He wanted to boast. He wanted to tell them that over the past month, his whole team figured out how to meet and exceed their goals, all while cutting expenses and becoming more excited than ever to come to work. But then he thought back to Robin, Adam, and Ricardo, the squirrels he'd met at the business district, and he decided to go a different way: "Actually, I've learned that my old approach was a mistake," he said, and everyone went quiet. Even the wind seemed to hold its breath and the willow tree stopped swaying. But Sam continued to speak into the quiet: "I guess I stuck with it because it made me feel powerful, and it got me results for a while. But I never considered at what cost. I didn't know I made everyone around me more stressed and less capable. I didn't realize I was draining power from my own organization. And when news of the condo development got out and we most needed the power to act, we didn't have enough power left to go around."

"So, what exactly are you saying?" Jose pressed. "That you stepped down as the leader?"

"Actually," said Sam, "I've finally stepped up. I'm still figuring it out, but I think I understand now that a leader's purpose is to be a catalyst. It's not my job to use my power to get things done but to grow the power of my team so we can all get more done together."

"Okay," said Eva slowly. "So, you're saying you started giving everyone around you more power, and it made your company even more successful?"

"Well, not right away," Sam said. And he laughed, thinking of the frantic conversation he'd had with his management team almost exactly one month earlier. "I made a lot of mistakes. I tried to do too many things, too quickly. Some things actually seemed to get worse at first. But then we brought our challenges to the team and found solutions together."

"Like what?" asked Jose.

"For example, we loosened our policies and gave everyone authority to make their own sales decisions," said Sam. "It created a lot of confusion and miscommunication. But then we asked our sales team how to fix it, and they created checkpoints to share feedback. It helped everyone align quickly while trying out lots of creative solutions for our customers."

"I do have to say," said Sylvio, "your new acorn necklaces are an ingenious way to keep the kids busy."

"Thank you," said Sam. "A small team of sales squirrels tried it out as an experiment, and now it's one of our best sellers."

"What else did you get wrong?" Jose asked (a little too eagerly).

"We also launched way too many task forces too quickly. It stretched us in too many directions, and it stretched our employees too thin. Some of them started to feel resentful because they were basically doing free labor."

"So how did you fix it?" asked Eva.

"We didn't," said Sam. "We took the challenge to our task force members and asked for their advice. They helped us decide which task forces to pause and taught us how to set them up better. Now we know to clarify that the power to contribute doesn't mean the *obligation* to contribute. And we found ways to reduce workload by 15 percent so task force members actually had time to participate. Thanks to our task forces we now have a new way to store more acorns longer, and we have a system to communicate more quickly across our entire branch."

"Sounds a little too chaotic for my taste," said Jose.

"Oh, it was at first," Sam agreed. "We basically asked everyone to get involved in everything all at once. Some squirrels were upset because we invited their feedback but didn't act on all of it. So, we learned not to ask until we were ready to take action. And we got better at setting expectations around how we'll use each other's input."

"So it's going well now?" asked Eva. And Sam paused to consider her question so he could answer honestly.

"I think it is," he said. "There were lots of bumps at first, but we stuck with it, kept learning, and figured out how to turn a new leaf together. The silos we used to have between departments melted away. And we got friends and families involved. My wife, Amara, has been a huge help."

"Great dentist," said Jose with an approving nod and a tap on his shiny white teeth, and the rest of the group murmured their agreement.

"Turns out she's also a great community organizer," said Sam. "She got all sorts of squirrels to help out with our nut-trition education campaign. Even our pups spread the word at school. Our sales shot up, and so did our community members' ability to prepare for the recession. Some squirrels on our team found ways to collaborate with other branches at our company, and some are even collaborating with our competitors."

There was another silence, and then Sylvio said, "Well, what the *shell*? Why don't we look into how *our* businesses could collaborate?" And for perhaps the first time in High Tails history, several members of the group actually asked each other for advice and looked for ways to help one another out.[30]

After the meeting, Sam made the commute back to his office. It had been a good meeting and a very good day. But for some reason, he couldn't help feeling a tinge of melancholy. He tried to shake it off. Then, when it didn't leave, he let himself wonder what it was. He realized he was missing Mary—not just Mary the wise guide by his side but also Mary the peculiar squirrel with the question-mark tail and the propensity to pun. He missed his friend.

He wished he could tell her everything he'd been learning. He wished he could ask her questions. He wished he could speak to the community's squirrel scientists and educators and business leaders and maybe even the magicians. He wished there was someone close by he looked up to who could give him advice. And just as this thought crossed his mind, Sam looked up to see Jack Walnuts dangling his feet off a tall branch.

Chapter 32

· · · · · · ·

A Job Offer

"Mr. Walnuts!" Sam exclaimed, and he realized he was entirely unprepared to see him. A tiny compartment of his mind had always been dedicated to anticipating a surprise visit from his boss. This small, stout squirrel with his wildfire tail was not just the chief nut officer of the company but also the living embodiment of everything Sam had wanted to be as a leader. Sam had tried to look at everything through two sets of eyes: his own and the critical gaze of the squirrel he aspired to become.

Only ever since he returned from Mary's community, he thought of Jack Walnuts less and less. At first, he kept expecting his boss to storm into the office and take over the entire operation or maybe even shut it down. He had fitful dreams in which Mr. Walnuts berated him, called him a phony, then fired him in front of everyone he knew. But as Sam seeded the power-with principles and watched them take root, the ever-burning image of Mr. Walnuts faded.

Now, having dropped down from his branch with a small but decisive thump, Jack Walnuts stood right before Sam with his copper tail poofed out in all its bushy glory.

"Hello, Samuel," said Mr. Walnuts in his gravelly voice.

"Mr. Walnuts!" Sam said again, because it was all he could think to say.

"Well, what did I tell you?" said Mr. Walnuts.

Sam's mind raced furiously with snippets of things Jack Walnuts had told him. Was it to bury your competition before they bury you? Was it to be the first one in and the last one out of the office every day? Was it to project confidence even when you don't have any? To assume your employees will always try to do less work and ask for more pay? To get the best squirrels into your tree and kick the rest off the branch? Or that thing about work-life balance being a scam? Or did he mean the classic "Know the way and make them go your way"?

"You've said so many things, sir," said Sam. Mr. Walnuts let out a sharp laugh and slapped him on the back.

"You're overthinking it, son," he said. "I told you it's the tough times that separate the real leaders from the phonies. Didn't I?"

"Right," said Sam. "You did say that."

It was the comment that had haunted Sam all the way into the darkest depths of the forest. It was the fear that ate away at him even when he wasn't thinking about it consciously. And the great irony, Sam understood now, was that trying to lead just like Jack Walnuts was actually the thing that had kept him from leading well. Even if Mr. Walnuts disagreed (and he almost definitely would), this was the first time Sam felt confident he was doing a good job. Was he a great leader? Maybe not quite yet. But he was learning every day. If he had to lose his job at Nuts for You because of his new approach, then so be it. He could never go back now.

"Then why do you look like you just bit into an empty peanut?" Mr. Walnuts barked. "Your branch is outperforming every other branch. Our brand's reputation is better than it's been in seasons. And I don't know what you've got going on at the office, but your squirrels actually look like they're having a good time."

"Oh," said Sam, "I mean, yes. Yes, we have a terrific team, sir. We've been able to get creative and overcome a whole lot of obstacles. We—"

"This ain't France, boy," Mr. Walnuts interrupted. "What's with all this *we we we*? I'm here to talk to *you*. I came to tell you I'm impressed by what you've done. And even more than that, I'm tired. I've been doing this too long, and my family has been pestering me to retire. So, if you want the job, it's yours."

"The job, sir?" Sam asked.

"Oh, quit pulling my tail, would you?" said Mr. Walnuts. "I'm talking about *the* job: the chief nut officer. I'm ready to give it, if you're ready to take it."

Sam's heart seemed to freeze in his chest, and then it began to thunder. His paws shook, and the pads of his feet became instantly sweaty. This is what he had wanted all along. This is what he had been working toward. So why hadn't he already said yes? Could it be somewhere along the way he stopped wanting it? Would accepting the job actually get in the way of his progress? Then again, what if he could put all that power to good use? It was power he could share with his team and his community. It was power they could grow together.

Before the fear of the forest recession became a constant in his life, any time Sam caught his reflection in a shiny surface, he tried out different facial expressions he could use for the moment Jack Walnuts finally gave him this job. How many different scenarios had he played out in his head? How many times had he practiced his acceptance speech? Yet somehow, all of those perfect words were gone now.

"I'm ready," Sam heard himself say.

And then he heard Mr. Walnuts reply: "Good. Because the condo construction has been pushed up to next week."

Chapter 33

· · · · · · ·

The Acorn

Sam clutched the single acorn that remained from his meeting with Mary. It gave him the courage to walk into the meadow that held employees from all three branches of Nuts for You, Inc. He was responsible for all of them now. Or rather—he corrected himself—he was responsible *with* all of them. This crowd would have to become the community that would have to save their company, together. But could they actually do it in time? He had no idea.

"Look, there's Sam!" called Paloma, and a quiet settled over the meadow like fresh snow. It had been a long time since his presence had this effect, and Sam realized they'd have to rebuild the trust they'd established together at their branch across the entire company.

"It's great to meet you, Mr. Squirrel," said a nervous-looking tree squirrel who stood beside Paloma. "I'm the executive manager of our western branch."

"And I manage our eastern branch," said another squirrel with a not-so-subtle attempt to step in front of the western branch manager.

"Please call me Sam," said Sam. "I'm excited to work together and get to learn from you and your teams."

"Congrats on the promotion, Sam," said Paloma with a grin.

"And congrats on yours," Sam said. One of the first things his management team did with its newfound power was to finally give Paloma authority of her own. After all those years, she now not only had her informal power to run on but also formal power to make company-wide decisions too. Sam just hoped the company would exist long enough for that power to count.

"Sam, we all already know about the condo schedule change," said Mila, who had somehow transformed over the past few weeks from someone who chronically shielded her team to someone who constantly made them stronger.

"It's bad," said Francesca. "And another increase in our productivity won't solve our problems. But we're going to figure this out together." And Sam knew she actually meant it. She had been turning to her team in earnest, supporting their decisions, and integrating their ideas. Sure, she never gave up her big office, but she did let a group of squirrels use it to hold a retirement party for their six-year-old colleague.

"How about we start by going around and hearing everyone's questions? We can share what we know, then break off into cross-branch teams to come up with new ideas?" said Ravi, and Sam stared at him. This squirrel who used to do everything in his power to avoid using his power was now among the first to ask questions and offer suggestions. He rarely used his formal power to get things done anymore, but his informal power inspired squirrels to listen when he spoke, to help him, and to come to him for help.

"I think that sounds great," said Paloma.

And, over the next two days, that's exactly what they did. But no matter how hard they tried or how long they worked, no one could find an idea that would get their business out of danger. The condo construction grew nearer.

Human shouts broke through the trees into the forest, even in the dead of night. In the distance, they could hear the rumble of construction equipment preparing to do its work. More and more often, the ground trembled, sending branches and nests tumbling to the ground as creatures screamed and scurried away. How could they find a solution to protect their offices when they didn't even know if their offices would be left standing? How could they invent a way to house their inventory if they had no way to guess how much of their inventory would be left? Sam tried to cling to hope, but it slipped through his paws like water. And then someone proposed an idea.

Nathan was the first ground squirrel Nuts for You ever hired. He was also the first squirrel in his department with a background in history rather than business. It took him awhile to feel comfortable enough to speak up. But once he did, everything changed.

"Is it okay if I ask a question?" he said at the start of their daily company huddle. "That is, I mean other than that first one I just asked? And this one, I guess—"

"Just go ahead," said Paloma, giving Nathan a small nudge.

"Well, I guess I was wondering about our purpose," he said, so quietly that everyone had to strain their ears (which are already two-and-a-half times better at hearing than human ears). "We've said our purpose is to save the company. But, well, I wonder if it's actually our real purpose?"

"What do you mean?" asked the eastern branch manager. "What other purpose is there?"

"Well," said Nathan, "I guess I ask because I think if we try to preserve our company as it is now, we probably won't find a solution in time." A murmur passed through the group. Paloma nudged Nathan again to continue. "But I think maybe if we try to achieve the real purpose behind our company, then we may have a way to do it."

"To feed the squirrels in our forest," said Sam quietly, remembering his own epiphany back at the community's business district.

"What?" asked Francesca.

"Nathan is right. That's our real purpose," said Sam. "If we can achieve that purpose, then it doesn't matter what our company becomes or even whether it continues to exist at all."

Sam looked around and saw heads nodding and tails swishing. A warmth spread among them he could only describe as being one community with one shared purpose.

"Well, if that's true," Nathan went on with a bit more conviction, "then I think we squirrels may actually be at the heart of the solution."

"What does that mean?" someone called from the back.

"Yeah! Tell us more!" called another voice. And the group seemed to move as one to form a large circle of squirrels so they could hear and see one another at the same time. Sam felt himself dissolve into the circle and smiled, knowing that a passerby would never be able to tell who was in charge of what. They'd have no choice but to pay attention to and respect each of them equally.

"Have you ever found a great spot to bury your stash, only to forget where you hid it later?" asked Nathan. A knowing laugh rippled through the circle. "Well, it turns out that's how thousands of trees in our forest came to exist. Most nut trees are actually planted by squirrels. I guess nuts are a whole lot like power. The more of them you give away, the more they grow." Another sound rippled through the circle—this time, a swell of different reactions.

"That's great," said one squirrel, "but nut trees take entire generations to grow. Sure, we'd be helping future squirrels, but how do we help ourselves now?"

"Two words," said the eastern branch manager: "Hazel. Nuts."

"That's one word!" cried the western branch manager.

"My point is, they grow faster than any other nut tree. That can be where we start."

"Easy for a three-year-old to say," someone scoffed. "Some of us don't have years to sit around waiting for our dinner."

"Well, maybe we can diversify our offerings and start planting more than just nuts," said Ravi. "We can plant mushrooms. We can plant berries."

"And we can plant acorns for all the squirrels and other animals who come after us," said Sam.

"It would mean branching out into other parts of the forest," said Francesca.

"We'd have to find ways to collaborate with everyone who already lives there," said Mila. "Maybe we can even rebrand as Nuts Together!"

"It will be a whole lot of change," said Paloma.

"Yes, it will," said Sam, and then he remembered his friend and said, "And so long as we can change, we can overcome anything that comes our way."

After the meeting, Sam climbed up to the room that used to be his office and finally pulled open his beloved safe. The acorns bounced, knocked, and tumbled out onto the floor. Instead of going out to gather, Sam decided to spend the rest of his day planting these seeds. Perhaps his family would join too, so he and Amara could show their pups what it really takes to be a leader: the courage to lead together. Perhaps if they ventured far enough, they'd even run into his friend with the perpetual question-mark tail and invite her community to join their quest.

It was all so scary, so big, and so overwhelming, but Sam knew exactly how he would start. He took the small acorn he'd brought home from the power-with community and placed it gingerly atop the pile. This would be the first acorn he'd plant.

POWER-WITH PLANNING

You've now reached the end of Sam's story, but your own story is just beginning. Take a moment to review the insights from the last leg of Sam's journey, then apply them to your own challenges:

- It can be tempting to take a power-over approach to putting power-with principles in action. Instead, align on a shared purpose, ask questions to understand the context behind people's concerns, and explore solutions to integrate people's perspectives.
- Instead of deciding on power-with tactics alone, gather and apply input from others.
- Start small. Decide on one time-bound, safe-to-try experiment to implement first.
- Set checkpoints in advance to reflect on how your experiment is going, and make adjustments to the plan, if needed.

CHECK-IN QUESTIONS: YOUR STORY

- *Now that you've gotten to see Sam's transformation, consider your own. How have your beliefs and behaviors changed since we first crossed paths?*

- *What is the before-and-after story you want to tell about your challenges and how you will have faced them?*

- *What is the first power-with seed you will plant?*

··· POWER-WITH SUMMARY ···

Want a refresher of the ideas in this book or an easy way to talk about power with others? Here are the most important insights and terms . . . in a nutshell.

Power-With Objective: What are the goals a power-with model helps us achieve?

These days, organizations need teams that are more effective, inspired, and resilient than ever. The key to achieving this state of ever-expanding organizational capability is building a power-with organization.

A power-with company is one that:

- Is **nimble** enough to adjust to unexpected obstacles and opportunities and achieve results in the midst of rapid change.
- Quickly produces **innovative ideas** and solutions thanks to systems and a culture that enables creativity and rapid learning.
- Is a place where people want to work and an environment that contributes to individual and collective **flourishing**.

Power-With Strategy: How can we achieve these goals?

The core strategy for building an organization with increasing capacity to achieve its mission while fostering an inspired environment is to foster a power-with ecosystem.

A power-with model relies on two practices that expand power while keeping it in balance:

1. Grow people's personal power (formal authority and informal influence).
2. Distribute power so it's not too concentrated with any person or group.

4 Power-With Principles: How can we bring this strategy to life?

The following four power-with principles help generate ideas to balance power and lead together well.

1. **Follow a purpose, not a person**.
- **What it is:** Make decisions to achieve a shared purpose rather than to please a person.
- **Why it matters to the organization:** A clear purpose lets everyone progress toward the same goal, reduces bottlenecks, and places less strain on leaders.
- **Why it matters to the person:** It creates a feeling of clarity, meaning, and progress.
- **Beliefs behind the principle:**
  ○ People want to make meaningful contributions to a mission that moves them.
  ○ Commitment to a cause produces better results than compliance to orders.

- o An overreliance on leaders leaves organizations vulnerable.
- **Drawbacks to the alternative:**
  - o At best, following a person (rather than a purpose) creates confusion and disengagement and slows down progress as people wait for orders.
  - o At worst, it stops people from speaking up because they fear authority.
- **Common challenges:**
  - o Aligning on a clear purpose often requires more time and effort up front.
  - o A major change in purpose can threaten commitment.
- **How to overcome them:**
  - o Use tools that help you create clarity efficiently (you can find some at TaniaLuna.com).
  - o Set expectations that purpose may change over time if the situation changes.

2. Rely on context, not control.

- **What it is:** Clarify the *why* rather than dictating the *how*.
- **Why it matters to the organization:** It lets people move quickly, independently, and joyfully, while making well-informed decisions.
- **Why it matters to the person:** It results in a sense of choice, freedom, and ownership over one's own work.

- **Beliefs behind the principle:**
  - ○ Autonomy is a key driver of engagement and creativity.
  - ○ Most people are trustworthy, and feeling trusted results in more thoughtful, responsible decisions.
  - ○ The cost of betrayed trust is usually lower than the cost of mistrusting.
- **Drawbacks to the alternative:** Feeling controlled reduces creativity, learning, and agility while increasing stress, and a lack of context limits decision-making quality.
- **Common challenges:**
  - ○ Too much autonomy can result in bad decisions or fear of deciding.
  - ○ It can be tough to judge the quality of people's decisions.
- **How to overcome them:**
  - ○ Expand scope of autonomy gradually and develop feedback checkpoints.
  - ○ Establish and track measurable success metrics.

3. Be a cultivator, not a collector.

- **What it is:** Focus on growing effectiveness rather than searching for ready-made talent.
- **Why it matters to the organization:** It equips teams with the ability to achieve their results now and in the face of change.
- **Why it matters to the person:** It allows for growth, learning, and self-efficacy.

- **Beliefs behind the principle:**
  - People have the ability and desire to learn and grow.
  - Diversity is a source of strength when people can leverage their differences.
  - Intrapersonal and interpersonal skills make teams stronger and more adaptive.
- **Drawbacks to the alternative:** Attempting to collect people from a small, finite crop of talent (rather than cultivating an infinite field) limits team capabilities and harms engagement, diversity, and equity on an organizational and societal level.
- **Common challenges:**
  - It can result in an overreliance on your existing team.
  - It can be tricky to distinguish poor role fit from a lack of sufficient development, resulting in delayed termination decisions.
- **How to overcome them:**
  - Promote open roles internally and externally.
  - Offer resources to develop skills quickly and set target timelines for achieving results within a role.

4. Build a community, not a crowd.

- **What it is:** Invite people to cocreate your team rather than act as passive participants.
- **Why it matters to the organization:** Participation in org-level decisions leads to better decisions and higher commitment.

- **Why it matters to the person:** It increases satisfaction with, pride in, and passion for one's work and workplace.
- **Beliefs behind the principle:**
  - An owner mindset leads to a sense of commitment, belonging, and engagement.
  - People feel they own something when they've played a role in building it.
  - An organization is strongest when people participate in its design and direction.
- **Drawbacks to the alternative:** Working in an impersonal crowd (rather than in an interconnected community) causes distance, mistrust, and inefficiency.
- **Common challenges:**
  - Participation can be time-consuming or exhausting, or it can distract people from their primary roles and responsibilities.
  - It can result in resentment if contributions aren't used or valued.
- **How to overcome them:**
  - Start small, and clarify that participation is optional rather than expected.
  - Set aside paid time to contribute so it doesn't turn into volunteer labor.
  - Clarify how (and whether) all contributions will be used.

Key Concepts: What else is important to know about power?

- **Power is the capacity to get things done** (e.g., solve a problem, reach a goal, meet a need). More power means fewer limits on what an individual or team can achieve. It's possible to have power without having the responsibility to use that power. Responsibility means having the obligation to use one's power.
- **Power comes from** control over access to scarce and valuable resources—especially those that increase safety or self-esteem—or the ability to take resources away.
- **Personal power** refers to the capacity of an individual.
- **Collective power** refers to the capacity of a group.
- **To grow personal and collective capacity,** we need a balance of power. If an individual has too little or too much power, the group suffers and, often, so does the individual.
- **Sudden access to power** can create feelings of uncertainty, insecurity, and isolation. When we feel a sense of social connection and support, using our power feels safer.
- **Feeling powerful** increases proactivity, creativity, and willingness to share our perspectives.
- **Feeling powerless** produces stress, inaction, withdrawal, and even health problems.
- **Having too much** power can reduce our empathy and increase our odds of taking thoughtless risks, making mistakes, and breaking rules.

- **Formal power** comes from official authority. To be sustainable, it must be granted voluntarily.
- **Informal power** comes from earning influence. Usually, people can get more accomplished when they have informal and formal power combined.
- **The following power profiles** describe common approaches to using power. They are not fixed character traits but acquired styles that can change over time:
  - **Power-over** refers to using power to control others or to limit their power.
    - **Power grabber** is a power-over style characterized by striving to acquire ever more authority. This approach is unapologetic about taking control and giving orders.
    - **Power masker** is a style that seems empowering on the surface but masks a power-over approach with questions or options that are veiled orders.
    - **Power sapper** is another power-over style, characterized by protecting people from the strain and stress of responsibility, thereby making them even less powerful.
  - **Power shrugger** is a power-under style in which people avoid making decisions or taking responsibility in the hope that someone else will do it for them.
  - **Power-with** refers to using our personal power to increase others' power, which, in turn, increases our own. By lifting up the group, we ultimately lift up ourselves.

Your Insights: What else do you want to remember about what you read?

Jot down notes for your future self here:

··· POWER-WITH TACTICS AND TOOLS ···

Ready to start putting power-with ideas into action? Below is your personal treasure chest-*nut* of ideas and tools to get started. For bonus resources, templates, assessments, and an opportunity to join a community with other power-with people, go to TaniaLuna.com.

1. Follow a Purpose Not a Person: Powerful Ideas to Try	
Help your team make decisions to achieve a shared purpose rather than to please a person.	
To grow personal power	• Keep the organizational and team **purpose**, **objectives**, **strategy**, and **priorities** clear and visible to all.
	• Have a **small number of easy-to-remember priorities**.
	• Clarify each role's **purpose** and **success metrics.**
	• Give people visibility into the **impact** of their work.
	• Make **metric tracking** simple so people can assess their own results.

To dis- tribute power	• **Hire** and **promote** people who **value sharing power.**
	• Encourage and create opportunities for leaders to **model approachability** (e.g., tell personal stories, share mistakes).
	• Give people the ability to **select, assess,** and **remove leaders.**
	• Ensure that people with formal authority do not break **norms or rules.**
	• Limit your number of **leadership levels.**
	• Remove or rotate **status symbols** (e.g., parking, fancy offices).

Get tools and templates to clarify organizational and role purpose at TaniaLuna.com.

2. Rely on Context, Not Control: Powerful Ideas to Try
Make sure everyone knows the why *so you don't have to dictate the* how.

To grow personal power	• Give **easy access to information** that can influence how people do their work (e.g., budget, decision criteria). • Offer education on **how to use the information** (e.g., how to interpret P&L report, why a metric matters), and check for understanding. • Clarify **roles**, **responsibilities**, and **decision-making authority** and how to resolve role **confusion.** • Create a norm of **sharing the reasoning** for requests, assignments, feedback, and decisions. • Where possible, give **people choice** over what they do and how they do it, or cocreate the plan.

To distribute power	• Eliminate or simplify **policies or rules** to allow for personal judgment (e.g., where to work, when to work, what to wear, when to take breaks, when to take time off).
	• Grant **decision-making authority** to people closest to the work rather than concentrating it with a small number of approvers.
	• Share information with everyone **at the same time**, especially among remote or physically distributed groups.
	• Replace power-over **terminology** (like "subordinates") with power-with terms (like "team") to reduce controlling ways of thinking.
Get tools and templates to clarify context and minimize control at TaniaLuna.com.	

3. Be a Cultivator, Not a Collector: Powerful Ideas to Try

Spend more time growing people's effectiveness than searching for ready-made talent.

To grow personal power	• Provide people with all the **resources** they need to achieve results.
	• Clarify the **skills and knowledge** people must have for each role.
	• Carve out time for people to **learn on the job.**
	• Support individual **skill-building**, including **(a)** role-specific expertise, **(b)** interpersonal skills (e.g., influence); and **(c)** intrapersonal skills (e.g., job crafting) within and even outside your team.
	• Offer different **learning modalities** to serve different learning needs.
	• **Ritualize feedback** conversations across all levels.
	• **Teach leaders** how to build up their team's skills and self-efficacy rather than solving all the problems themselves.
To distribute power	• Remove **unnecessary barriers to entry** for roles (e.g., don't use years of experience or a specific degree as hiring criteria).

To distribute power	• **Promote opportunities** to learn and grow to everyone at the same time, especially in remote and distributed environments.
	• Develop systems for **cross-training** so knowledge is well distributed.
	• Offer **supplemental learning** to individuals who have had less access to development opportunities in the past.
Get tools and templates to grow your team at TaniaLuna.com.	

4. Build a Community, Not a Crowd: Powerful Ideas to Try
Invite people to cocreate your team rather than act as passive participants.

To grow personal power	• Invite everyone to **play a role** in setting **goals** and **strategy.**
	• Provide **systems for contribution** (e.g., voting on decisions, proposing ideas, joining task forces, giving feedback).
	• Make sure everyone **knows how to participate** in cobuilding and cogoverning your team and knows the expectations of **good citizenship.**
	• **Set expectations** for how you will use input, who makes final decisions, and whether contributing is optional or required.
	• **Allocate time** for people to contribute and participate.
	• Ask team members to be **representatives** internally and externally.
	• Ritualize **team interactions** that improve collaboration and **connection** (e.g., retrospectives, celebrations, peer coaching, resource groups).
	• Share **profits,** equity, or both, so employees are true owners.

To distri- bute power	• Establish a **norm of involving voices** from those with different roles, identities, and perspectives, including anyone impacted by a decision.
	• Set an **equal turn-taking** norm in meetings and group interactions.
	• Have **two or more decision-makers** for high-stakes decisions (e.g., hiring, promotions, salary-setting, terminations).
	• **Rotate formal authority** (e.g., two-year terms for certain roles, different presenters at internal or external events).
	• Give everyone **access to people with power** (e.g., virtual office hours).

Get tools and templates to build your community
at TaniaLuna.com.

	Power-With Org Diagnostic *Not sure how to diagnose your own team or company? Here are the most common power-with vs. power-over differences at a glance.*	
	Power-with	**Power-over**
Mission & vision	- Cocreate it. - Keep it clear and accessible.	- Announce it. - Keep it in the leader's head.
Values	- Cocreate them. - Value sharing power. - Hold everyone to them.	- Announce them. - Value winning. - Give people with power a pass.
Strategy	- Cocreate it. - Keep it clear and accessible. - Check that all understand it.	- Announce it. - Keep it in the leader's head. - Assume no one needs to know.
Decision-making	- Have highly distributed authority. - Gather multiple perspectives. - Make decision criteria clear. - Explain reasons for decisions.	- Have highly concentrated authority. - Decide alone. - Let criteria live in the leader's head. - Announce new mandates.

	Power-with	Power-over
Org design	- Distribute authority. - Establish few levels of leadership. - Promote self-management. - Be adaptive and evolving. - Do highly cross-functional work. - Have few rules and policies.	- Make authority hierarchical. - Have many levels of leadership. - Require frequent supervision. - Be fixed and slow to change. - Do highly siloed work. - Have frequent need to get approval.
Leadership	- Set goals collaboratively. - Plan work collaboratively. - Promote mutual accountability. - Help people learn and grow. - Be accessible and approachable. - Catalyze team effectiveness. - Rely largely on influence.	- Have leaders define goals. - Have leaders assign tasks. - Have people report to managers. - Ensure people get work done. - Be intimidating or difficult to reach. - Define and direct work. - Rely largely on authority.

	Power-with	Power-over
Hiring & recruiting	- Assess based on observations. - View differences as an asset. - Apply standardized process. - Use diverse hiring sources. - Minimize barriers to entry. - Invite candidates' questions. - Have two-plus decision-makers.	- Assess based on résumé. - Focus on culture fit. - Follow gut instincts. - Rely only on personal network. - Require many qualifications. - Hold one-way interviews. - Let one person decide alone.
Work conditions	- Plan time off collaboratively. - Enable flexible work hours. - Enable flexible location.	- Let leaders approve time off. - Mandate work hours. - Require a fixed location.
Compen-sation	- Make criteria transparent. - Criteria are consistent. - Have two-plus decision-makers.	- Criteria live in leader's head. - Criteria are inconsistent. - Fate rests only in leader's hands.
Roles	- Roles focus on purpose. - Success metrics are clear. - Decision-making rights are clear. - Roles frequently updated. - Roles are rotated and shared.	- Roles focus on tasks. - No clear definition of success exists. - Decision-making rights are vague. - Roles quickly outdated. - Roles and titles are fixed.

	Power-with	**Power-over**
Growth & learning	- Focused on learning. - Value questions. - Learning is frequently peer-led. - Learning is cross-functional. - Feedback is multidirectional. - Prioritize developing skills.	- Focused on knowing. - Value answers. - Learning is exclusively top-down. - Learning is specialized and siloed. - Feedback is only top-down. - Prioritize hiring "A players."
Careers	- Focus on impact. - Opportunities promoted to all. - Career evolution is frequent and nonlinear. - People drive their own growth. - Promotion criteria are clear. - Two-plus evaluate promotions.	- Focus on prestige. - Opportunities known only to few. - Career evolution happens slowly and prescriptively. - People wait to be promoted. - Decisions are based on preference. - Leader is sole gatekeeper.
Performance assessment	- People can track own metrics. - Assessment is mutual. - Criteria are transparent. - Criteria are consistent. - Self-evaluations matter.	- Leader determines success. - Leader evaluates direct reports. - Criteria live in leader's head. - Criteria are inconsistent. - Leader evaluates alone.

	Power-with	Power-over
Employment terminations	- Criteria are transparent. - Criteria are consistent. - Two-plus people decide.	- Criteria live in leader's head - Criteria are inconsistent. - Leader decides alone.
Meetings	- Turn-taking is the norm. - Facilitator and notetaker rotate. - Agenda is cocreated. - Key info captured and shared.	- Loudest voices tend to dominate. - Meeting roles are fixed. - Agenda is set by leaders. - People must attend to stay informed.
Social connection	- Relationships are valued. - Time set to build relationships. - Connections are cross-functional. - Relationships are deliberate.	- Relationships seen as nice to have. - Socializing happens off the clock. - Interactions are siloed. - Interactions are accidental.
Organizational participation	- All can weigh in on org decisions. - Ideas come from anywhere. - Giving feedback is easy. - Workplace culture is co-owned. - Proposals are welcome. - Task forces are cross-functional. - Time to participate is designated.	- Org decisions made by leaders. - Ideas come from designated roles. - People stay in their lane. - Norms and systems are mandated. - Orders come from above. - Work gets done within silos. - Contributions are volunteer time.
Download this diagnostic at TaniaLuna.com.		

Power-With Assessment

Not sure where to start your power-with journey? There is no one right (or wrong) way to go, and even small changes can have a big impact. That said, it helps to hear from your team so you can pick a path together.

You'll find two questionnaire options below to help you gather your team's perspectives. Change the wording from company *to* team *or* department, *depending on your focus. You can down-load these questionnaires at TaniaLuna.com.*

Quick Questionnaire

1. The kind of power I most value *already having* at our company is:
2. The kind of power I'd like to have *more* of at our company is:
3. What already makes me feel like an important part of our company is:
4. What would make me feel a greater sense of ownership here is:
5. How distributed is power at our company, on a scale of 1–5, where 1 represents a small number of people holding power and 5 represents all people holding power?

Complete Questionnaire

Please answer on a scale of 1–5
(1 = strongly disagree, 5 = strongly agree):

Follow a Purpose, Not a Person

1. I know our company mission and vision (why we exist and what we aim to achieve).
2. I understand our overall company strategy (how we plan to achieve our vision).
3. At any given time, I know our priorities (what is most important for our company).
4. I understand the purpose of my role.
5. I understand how success is measured for my role.
6. I am able to track my own progress against my goals.
7. I can see the impact of my work and why it matters.
8. People at our company value sharing power with each other.
9. People at our company rely on influence rather than authority to achieve results.
10. People with formal authority at our company are held to the same standards as everyone else (no one is above the law).
11. It's possible to share feedback with people who have power at our company without fear of negative consequences.
12. There are few status symbols at our company (you wouldn't be able to tell who has more or less authority here unless someone told you).

Rely on Context, Not Control

13. I have access to the information I need to make high-quality decisions.
14. All people have equal access to important information that's relevant to their work.
15. I know how to interpret the information my company shares with me.
16. I understand the criteria for how important decisions are made at our company.
17. When people make requests or decisions here, they share the relevant context.
18. I have a good understanding of other people's roles, responsibilities, and decision-making authority.
19. I'm satisfied with how much freedom I have to do my work.
20. I have the decision-making authority I need to do my work well.
21. My job offers me the flexibility I need.

Be a Cultivator, Not a Collector

22. I have the resources I need to achieve my goals.
23. I know what skills and knowledge I need to achieve my goals.
24. My company helps me develop the skills I need to do my work well.
25. I receive timely, high-quality feedback on my work.
26. I am satisfied with how much I am learning and growing at work.

27. When there are opportunities for promotion or contribution, I know about them.
28. My coworkers and I regularly document and share our knowledge.
29. At our company, we remove unnecessary barriers to roles and opportunities (e.g., we don't require skills or experiences that aren't essential to do good work).

Build a Community, Not a Crowd
30. At our company, we gather diverse voices and perspectives before making a decision.
31. We make space to hear from everyone equally in meetings and group interactions.
32. I have easy access to people at my company who hold formal power.
33. My company makes it easy for me to play a role in shaping our internal systems, policies, processes, and culture.
34. My company makes it easy for me to play a role in influencing the direction of our company (such as our objectives or the tactics we select).
35. When I have an idea or feedback for our company, I know how to share it.
36. When I share my opinions at work, they really seem to count.
37. Making contributions at my company is a rewarding experience.

38. I feel comfortable using my power (e.g., freedom, decision-making authority) at work.
39. When there are high-stakes decisions to make at my company (e.g., hiring, termination), we involve multiple decision-makers.
40. We rotate who has formal power (e.g., who makes decisions, who leads meetings).
41. We distribute power across many people rather than keeping it concentrated with a small group of individuals.
42. I feel a sense of ownership within our company.

Short-Answer Questions
43. The kind of power I most value *already having* at our company is:

44. The kind of power I'd like to have *more* of at our company is:

45. Is there anything else you'd like to share?

··· INSPIRATION ···

Many individuals shaped my thinking about power, both consciously and unconsciously. The people who played a central role in influencing my beliefs made their way into this book as the following cast of characters:

Jack Walnuts, inspired by Jack Welch (and others)
The Chief Nut Officer of Nuts for You, Inc., is an amalgamation of many different leaders, but GE's longtime CEO Jack Welch played the most prominent role among them in shaping my worldview.

When I was first becoming interested in organizational psychology, Welch was heralded as an example of excellent leadership. Sure, over one hundred thousand people lost their jobs during his tenure, and he left GE unprepared to handle the dot-com bubble burst. But so many people still admired and emulated his methods.

He had a laser focus on "winning" and growing profits at all costs. He emphasized the importance of hiring the "right" people. And he popularized the rank-and-yank system that regularly pitted employees against each other and dumped the bottom 10 percent of "underperformers"—classic power-over moves.

As I learned more about Welch's methods, it occurred to me that just because a practice is common, it doesn't mean that it's right. He (inadvertently) helped grow my skepticism and got me into the habit of questioning what we accept as normal in business and in life.

For further reading, see David Gelles, *The Man Who Broke Capitalism: How Jack Welch Gutted the Heartland and Crushed the Soul of Corporate America—and How to Undo His Legacy* (New York: Simon & Schuster, 2022).

Alfie Akorn, inspired by Alfie Kohn (featured in the book with his permission)

If Jack Welch's bad behavior opened the door just a crack to show me how problematic popular business practices could be, the author and educator Alfie Kohn flung that door wide open.

Kohn's writing focuses on the ways we use power to control behavior in schools, workplaces, and relationships and how that control diminishes our individual and collective capacity to thrive. I came across his brilliant (and brutally honest) books when I was teaching psychology at Hunter College and looking for ways to give my students more power in the classroom. Thanks to him, I began to cocreate my curriculum with my class, support peer-to-peer learning, gather and apply feedback, and create the kind of environment my students actually needed to be able to learn.

Kohn also helped me see the power-over paradigm lurking beneath widely accepted practices like merit pay, incentive prizes, and even praise. And his call for "working *with*, rather than doing *to*" influenced all my actions as an educator, leader, and (I hope) human.

For further reading, see these Alfie Kohn books: Alfie Kohn, *Punished by Rewards: The Trouble with Gold Stars, Incentive Plans, A's, Praise, and Other Bribes*, 25th anniv. ed. (Boston: Mariner

Books, 2018); Alfie Kohn, *No Contest: The Case against Competition: Why We Lose in Our Race to Win*, rev. ed. (1986; Boston: Houghton Mifflin, 1992). Other books by Kohn are listed at https://www.AlfieKohn.org.

Tiziana Cashewrow and Julie Bats, inspired by Tiziana Casciaro and Julie Battilana (featured with their permission, input, and even some help coming up with their character names)

Even though power plays an important role in just about everyone's life every day, somehow the very concept of power remains both intimidating and elusive. Scholar-educators Casciaro and Battilana have made power more accessible through their writing, in more ways than one.

Not only do they simplify the complexity of what it is and how it works, but they also make the case that everyone can grow their power. They find a beautiful balance between addressing the entrenched and damaging ways in which power is distributed around the world and the practical steps anyone can take to reshape the status quo.

For further reading, see Julie Battilana and Tiziana Casciaro, *Power, for All: How It Really Works and Why It's Everyone's Business* (New York: Simon & Schuster, 2021).

Erich Furmm, inspired by Erich Fromm

Fromm was a social psychologist, therapist, and philosopher who shone an important light on our complex relationship with freedom. How could it be, he wondered—especially in light of World War II events—that we yearn for the power to take control of our lives, then willingly give it up when the weight of that responsibility gets too heavy?

He recognized that in times of fear and uncertainty, it can be all too comforting to trade in our personal power for the mindless guidance of conformity or authority. But Fromm pointed out that just because a child is scared to make decisions, it doesn't mean the child shouldn't grow up. He urged people to develop an inner freedom that grants us the sense of security we need to be able to use our own power.

For further reading, see Fromm's seminal book: Erich H. Fromm, *Escape from Freedom* (New York: Holt Reinhart and Winston, 1941; New York: Holt Paperbacks, 1969). See also Amy C. Edmondson, *The Fearless Organization: Creating Psychological Safety in the Workplace for Learning, Innovation, and Growth* (Hoboken, NJ: John Wiley & Sons, 2019).

Dasher Keltner: Inspired by Dacher Keltner (transformed into a prairie dog scientist with his permission)
Psychologist Dacher Keltner literally wrote the book on power. His creative experiments along with his compelling insights from other academic research sparked my fascination with the psychology of power and bolstered my conviction that our workplace and world would be better places for all with a better balance of power.

Keltner explores the harmful impacts of powerlessness on people's workplace contributions, well-being, and health, along with the freeing experience of feeling powerful. He describes the psychological state of having too much power as a kind of acquired psychopathy that inhibits our brains' capacity for empathy. And he famously describes the power paradox: doing what's best for others earns us power, but once we amass too much, we care more about ourselves and less about others.

For further reading, see Dacher Keltner, *The Power Paradox: How We Gain and Lose Influence* (New York: Penguin Books, 2017). Also listen to his interview in Adam Grant's audiobook: Adam Grant, *Power Moves: Lessons from Davos* (Newark, NJ: Audible, 2018), audio ed., 3 hrs., 3 min. See also: research led by psychologist Adam Galinsky, another leading researcher on the topic of power.

Peater Tree Coleman: Inspired by Peter T. Coleman (featured in the book with his permission)

As a social psychologist, Coleman studies how power shows up in many domains, such as interpersonal conflict, negotiation, leadership, political polarization, and international peace. He points out that the nature of power is dynamic, constantly shifting, constantly moving. It changes people and is therefore changed *by* people. Contrary to popular perception, Coleman makes the case that there's no such thing as a single best way to use our power but rather emphasizes the value of staying flexible with our style. In some cases, we may even need to take an occasional power-over or power-under stance to get the results we need.

Unlike most of her other beneficiaries, Coleman has been diligent in citing Mary Parker Follett among his influences and bringing her ideas into modern-day consciousness. As his student and my friend, Roi Ben-Yehuda (who introduced me to Coleman and Follett's scholarship) says, "We're all members of the I love Mary club."

For further reading, see Peter T. Coleman and Robert Ferguson, *Making Conflict Work: Harnessing the Power of Disagreement* (Boston: Mariner Books, 2015).

Robin Walnut Karrier: Inspired by Robin Wall Kimmerer
Robin Wall Kimmerer is a botanist, educator, essayist, and founder of the Center for Native Peoples and the Environment. In her writing, she weaves together scientific and Indigenous traditions in a way that transformed how I saw the world around me.

Through Kimmerer's eyes, all relationships between living beings are reciprocal and all flourishing is mutual. Asters and goldenrods attract more pollinators when they grow side by side. Humans are not doomed to strip the Earth of all resources but, instead, have the capacity to help trees, animals, and perhaps even other humans grow stronger together.

For further reading, see Robin Wall Kimmerer, *Braiding Sweetgrass: Indigenous Wisdom, Scientific Knowledge and the Teachings of Plants* (Minneapolis: Milkweed Editions, 2013); Robin Wall Kimmerer, *Gathering Moss: A Natural and Cultural History of Mosses* (Corvallis, OR: Oregon State University Press, 2003). See also Daniel Quinn, *Ishmael*, 25th anniv. ed. (New York, Bantam Books, 2017); Richard Powers, *The Overstory* (New York: W. W. Norton, 2018).

Adam Pomogrant: Inspired by Adam Grant (featured in the book with his permission)
Adam Grant is a perpetually insightful educator and psychologist. Once upon a time, like the prairie dog character he inspired in the book, he was also a professional magician.

Grant's first book explored the surprising dynamic of givers and takers in the workplace. To sum up his research through the lens of power, he found that the people most likely to succeed at work were neither the takers who didn't give (power-over) nor givers who didn't take (power-under). The people who earned the most trust, influence, and capacity to get things done were those who helped others *and* themselves (power-with). They shared their power in a way that strengthened others without depleting their own strength.

Reading his book along with his other research in organizational psychology felt like a sigh of relief I didn't know I needed. His insights taught me how to claw my way back from the edge of "giving burnout" and left me with more hope for the workplace and the world.

For further reading, see Adam Grant, *Give and Take: Why Helping Others Drives Our Success* (New York: Penguin, 2014); Adam Grant, *Power Moves: Lessons from Davos* (Newark, NJ: Audible, 2018), audio ed., 3 hrs., 3 min.

Ricardo Seedler: Inspired by Ricardo Semler

Though I've never had the pleasure of meeting Ricardo Semler, I feel like I know him. Maybe it's the delightfully familiar style of his books. Or it's the surprising discovery that we came to so many of the same conclusions across the span of different continents and decades. Or perhaps it's the fact that his approach to organizational design reminds me to keep work feeling fun.

Semler took over his father's traditional, hierarchical business in Brazil and transformed it into a shared power ecosystem, able to adapt to and withstand the harshest of political and economic conditions. He became a vocal advocate for distributed decision-making and minimal management. By the 1980s, he implemented practices (like remote work and role sharing) that were revolutionary then and are just catching on now. He was a proponent for keeping companies—or at least branches—under 150 people to allow for community-building and self-governance. And just as Sam Squirrel did in the book, he gave up his fancy office for employee meetings and birthday parties.

At some points, our philosophies diverge. For example, Semler does not believe in articulating mission, vision, or values so that they don't create restrictions or rigidity. I can appreciate the concern but have seen the opposite in practice. I'm also wary of his recommendation for self-set pay because I suspect it can perpetuate pay gaps, but I'm curious to learn more. Our similarities deepen my confidence in the power-with way, and our differences remind me there are no hard and fast rules to follow.

For further reading, see Ricardo Semler, *Maverick: The Success Story Behind the World's Most Unusual Workplace* (New York: Warner Books, 1995). See SemcoStyle.com for further learning.

Carol Dweckdini: Inspired by Carol Dweck
Dweck is a psychologist, researcher, and writer and another influence on how I teach, lead, and communicate. She shook up business, education, and probably a lot of other arenas too with her concept of the growth mindset.

Dweck and her collaborators describe a *fixed mindset* as a belief in our abilities being innate and largely incapable of change. This thinking leads companies to prioritize hiring the "best talent" rather than figuring out how to bring out the best in people. A fixed mindset also leads to less learning and risk-taking, since looking bad is a sign of incompetence. A *growth mindset* is the belief that our abilities develop through our efforts. This paradigm helps people learn, experiment, seek feedback, and persist in the face of setbacks.

For further reading, see Carol Dweck, *Mindset: The New Psychology of Success*, updated ed. (New York: Ballantine Books, 2016).

Other Sources of Inspiration

Style

The narrative style of this book was inspired by various writers, most prominently the following:

- B. F. Skinner, with his fascinating novela, *Walden Two*
- Daniel Quinn, with his philosophical novel, *Ishmael*
- Socrates (in general) and Christopher Phillips (and his book, *Socrates Cafe,* in particular), with his dedication to keeping the Socratic method alive and well
- Eliyahu M. Goldratt and Jeff Cox and their business novel, *The Goal: A Process of Ongoing Improvement*
- The delightful and practical business parables of Patrick M. Lencioni, John Kotter, Ken Blanchard, and Spencer Johnson

Companies

Aside from my own workplace experiments at my companies, Surprise Industries, LifeLabs Learning, and Scarlet Spark, I've learned from the power-with experiments of many other companies, such as Morning Star, W. L. Gore & Associates, Buurtzorg, Semco, Buffer, Netflix, The Ready, Valve, Medium, Zappos, Patagonia, and Github.

Additional Reading

Along with the books I referenced earlier, many other works of nonfiction and fiction contributed to, or chipped away at, my worldview. You can find my complete reading list at www.TaniaLuna.com.

Mary Parker Forest: Mary Parker Follett

Of course, the most significant inspiration for this book is Mary Parker Follett. She was a respected philosopher and scholar within her lifetime (1868–1933), the first woman to present at the London School of Economics, and an organizational advisor to President Theodore Roosevelt. The leadership researcher Warren Bennis once said, "Just about everything written today about leadership and organizations comes from Mary Parker Follett's writings and lectures."

The more of her work I read, the more I came to believe that Bennis wasn't exaggerating. Follett inspired a focus on win-win solutions in negotiation literature, normalized the idea that conflict can be constructive, sparked a dedication to employee development, influenced diversity and collaboration as values in the workplace, popularized the concept of continuous improvement, and so much more—mostly without attribution to her writing.

Follett thought so deeply and wrote so eloquently that instead of attempting to summarize more of her ideas, I've designated the next section of this book to let you hear them directly from her.

FROM MARY,
... IN HER OWN WORDS ...

Plenty of Mary Parker Follett's ideas made their way into this book already, but the precise words she used are so well-crafted that I want to share them with you here. The following direct quotations are from Mary Parker Follett's published works *Creative Experience* (1924) and *Dynamic Administration* (1941), and an excellent compilation of her philosophy, *Mary Parker Follett: Ideas We Need Today* by François Héon, Jennifer Jones-Patulli, Sébastien Damart, and Albie Davis.

On Diversity

"Fear of difference is dread of life itself."

"Evil is non-relation. That is, evil does not reside in this person or that person, but in the fact they are cut off from one another. If, as fellow citizens on Earth, we put this thought into action, we might let go of the ultimately dangerous definition of differences, one that allows us to set aside our shared humanity and instead sort people into categories where some are good and others are evil."

"As long as we think of difference as that which divides us, we shall dislike it; when we think of it as that which unites us, we shall cherish it."

On Integrating Our Differences

"We could not have an enemy unless there was much in common between us. Differences are always grounded in an underlying similarity."

"I remember, with humiliation, that we have fought because it is the easy way."

"From war to peace is not from the strenuous to the easy existence; it is from the futile to the effective, from the stagnant to the active, from the destructive to the creative way of life."

On Learning

"Education therefore is not chiefly to teach children a mass of things which have been true up to the present moment; moreover it is not to teach them to learn about life as fast as it is made, not even to interpret life, but above and beyond everything, to create life for themselves. Hence education should be largely the training in making choices. The aim of all proper training is not rigid adherence to a crystallized right (since in ethics, economics or politics there is no crystallized right), but the power to make a new choice at every moment."

"Citizenship is not to be learned in good government classes or current events courses or lessons in civics. It is to be acquired only through those modes of living and acting which shall teach us how to grow the social consciousness. This should be the object of all day school education, of all night school education, of all our supervised recreation, of all our family life, of our club life, of our civic life."

On Leadership

"The leader guides the group and is at the same time himself guided by the group, is always a part of the group. No one can truly lead except from within. One danger of conceiving the leader as outside is that then what ought to be group loyalty will become personal loyalty. When we have a leader within the group these two loyalties can merge."

"I believe we shall soon think of the leader as one who can organize the experience of the group, make it all available and most effectively available, and thus get the full power of the group. It is by organizing experience that we transform experience into power. And that is what experience is for, to be made into power."

"This means that some people are beginning to conceive of the leader, not as the man in the group who is able to assert his individual will and get others to follow him, but as the one who knows how to relate these different wills so that they will have a driving force. He must know how to create a group power rather than to express a personal power. He must make the team. The power of leadership is the power of integrating. This is the power which creates community."

"If the old idea of leader was the man with compelling personality, the idea today is the man who is the expression of a harmonious and effective unity which he has helped to form and which he is able to make a going affair. We no longer think that the best leader is the greatest hustler or the most persuasive orator or even the best trader. The great leader is he who is able to integrate the experience of all and use it for a common purpose."

"The best leader does not ask people to serve him, but the common end. The best leader has not followers, but men and women working with him. When we find that the leader does less than order and the expert more than advise, subordinates—both executives and workers—will respond differently to leadership. We want to arouse not the attitudes of obedience, but the attitudes of co-operation, and we cannot do that effectively unless we are working for a common purpose understood and defined as such."

"Our job is not how to get people to obey orders, but how to devise methods by which we can best *discover* the order integral to a particular situation. When that is found, the employee can issue it to the employer, as well as employer to employee."

"One *person* should not give orders to another *person*, but both should agree to take their orders from the situation."

"The best leaders get their orders obeyed because they too are obeying. Sincerity more than aggressiveness is a quality of leadership."

"Such a leader is not one who wishes to do people's thinking for them, but one who trains them to think for themselves."

"But the great leader tries also to develop power wherever he can among those who work with him, and then he gathers all this power and uses it as the energising force of a progressing enterprise."

"The person who influences me most is not he who does great deeds but he who makes me feel I can do great deeds."

"The community leader is he who can liberate the greatest amount of energy in his community."

"Our officials in their campaign speeches say that they are the 'servants of the people.' But we do not want 'servants' any more than we want bosses; we want genuine leaders."

"Loyalty to following The Invisible Leader gives us the strongest possible bond of union, establishes a sympathy which is not a sentimental but a dynamic sympathy."

"The object of a committee meeting is first of all to create a common idea. I do not go to a committee meeting merely to give my own ideas. If that were all, I might write my fellow-members a letter."

"For a good many years now we have been dominated by the crowd school, by the school which taught that people met together are governed by suggestion and imitation, and less notice has been taken of all the interplay which is the real social process that we have in a group but not in a crowd."

"The crowd often deadens thought because it wants immediate action, which means an unthinking unanimity not a genuine collective thought."

"When we hear it stated as a commonplace of human affairs that combined action is less intelligent than individual action, we must point out that it all depends upon whether it is a crowd combination or a group combination."

"The strength of the group does not depend on the greatest number of strong men, but on the strength of the bond between them, that is, on the amount of solidarity, on the best organization."

"I never react to you but to you-plus-me; or to be more accurate, it is I-plus-you reacting to you-plus-me. 'I' can never influence 'you' because you have already influenced me; that is, in the very process of meeting, by the very process of meeting, we both become something different. It begins even before we meet, in the anticipation of meeting."

"The most important thing to remember about unity is that there is no such thing. There is only unifying. You cannot get unity and expect it to last a day or five minutes."

On Power

"Genuine power can only be grown, it will slip from the every arbitrary hand that grasps it; for genuine power is not coercive control, but coactive control. Coercive power is the curse of the universe; coactive power, the enrichment and advancement of every human soul."

"I trust that the difference between this 'equal power,' so much talked of, and the power-with we have been considering, is evident. Equal power means the stage set for a fair fight, power-with is a jointly developing power, the aim, a unifying which, while allowing for infinite differing, does away with fighting."

"If your business is so organized that you can influence a co-manager while he is influencing you, so organized that a workman has an opportunity of influencing you as you have of influencing him; if there is an interactive influence going on all the time between you, power-with may be built up."

"Throughout history we see that control brings disastrous consequences whenever it outruns integration."

"We certainly do not want to abolish power, that would be abolishing life itself, but we need a new orientation toward it. The power of the strong is not to be used to conquer the weaker: this means for the conquerors activity which is not legitimately based, which will therefore have disastrous consequences later; and for the conquered, repression."

"We are part of a nation only in so far as we are helping to make that nation."

··· NOTES ···

1. Story improves attention, learning retention, and influence (especially if we get absorbed in or transported by the narrative), See Melanie C. Green and Timothy C. Brock, "The Role of Transportation in the Persuasiveness of Public Narratives," *Journal of Personality and Social Psychology* 79, no. 5 (November 2000): 701–21, https://doi.org/10.1037/0022-3514.79.5.701; Corinna Oschatz and Caroline Marker, "Long-Term Persuasive Effects in Narrative Communication Research: A Meta-Analysis," *Journal of Communication* 70, no. 4 (April 1, 2020): 473–96, https://doi.org/10.1093/joc/jqaa017.

2. There are many definitions of power. I liked the simplicity of this one, by the political scientist Emmanuel Remi Aiyede.

3. The real-life study used an annoying fan to assess the impact of power on willingness to take action. See Adam D. Galinsky, Deborah H. Gruenfeld, and Joe C. Magee, "From Power to Action," *Journal of Personality and Social Psychology* 85, no. 3 (2003): 453–66, https://doi.org/10.1037/0022-3514.85.3.453.

4. Adam D. Galinsky et al., "Power Reduces the Press of the Situation: Implications for Creativity, Conformity, and Dissonance," *Journal of Personality and Social Psychology* 95, no. 6 (2008): 1450–66, https://doi.org/10.1037/a0012633.

5. For a thorough review of the power research referenced in this chapter, see Dacher Keltner, *The Power Paradox: How We Gain and Lose Influence* (New York: Penguin, 2017).

6. Keltner references this unpublished pilot study in his book *The Power Paradox*, involving cookies rather than wildflowers. Participants who felt powerful were more likely to grab the last cookie and make a mess while eating it. It's not clear whether these results would be replicated on a larger scale, but the study still provides a great visual of how power impacts our actions.

7. Keltner discusses these findings in an interview in the audiobook: Adam Grant, *Power Moves: Lessons from Davos* (Newark, NJ: Audible Originals, 2018), audio ed., 3 hr., 3 min.

8. Adam D. Galinsky et al., "Power and Perspectives Not Taken," *Psychological Science* 17, no. 12 (December 2006): 1068–74, https://doi.org/10.1111/j.1467-9280.2006.01824.x; Adam D. Galinsky, Derek D. Rucker, and Joe C. Magee, "Power and Perspective-Taking: A Critical Examination," *Journal of Experimental Social Psychology* 67 (November 2016): 91–92, https://doi.org/10.1016/j.jesp.2015.12.002.

9. Peter Kollock, Philip Blumstein, and Pepper Schwartz, "Sex and Power in Interaction: Conversational Privileges and Duties," *American Sociological Review* 50, no. 1 (February 1985): 34, https://doi.org/10.2307/2095338.

10. Cameron Anderson and Adam D. Galinsky, "Power, Optimism, and Risk-Taking," *European Journal of Social Psychology* 36, no. 4 (July/August 2006): 511–36, https://doi.org/10.1002/ejsp.324; Jennifer Whitson et al., "The Blind, Leading: How Power Reduces Awareness

of Constraints in the Environment," *Academy of Management Proceedings* 2012, no. 1 (July 2012): 15288, https://doi.org/10.5465/ambpp.2012.15288abstract.

11. Fiske, Susan T. Fiske, "Controlling Other People: The Impact of Power on Stereotyping," *American Psychologist* 48, no. 6 (1993): 621–28. https://doi.org/10.1037/0003-066x.48.6.621.

   Susan Fiske proposes a helpful explanation for the relationship between power and the tendency to stereotype. With more power comes less incentive to pay attention to others, making people resort to snap judgements, thereby perpetuating power inequities in society.

12. David Dubois, Derek D. Rucker, and Adam D. Galinsky, "Social Class, Power, and Selfishness: When and Why Upper and Lower Class Individuals Behave Unethically," *Journal of Personality and Social Psychology* 108, no. 3 (2015): 436–49, https://doi.org/10.1037/pspi0000008; Yongmei Liu et al., "How Do Power and Status Differ in Predicting Unethical Decisions? A Cross-National Comparison of China and Canada," *Journal of Business Ethics* 167, no. 4 (2020): 745–60, https://doi.org/10.1007/s10551-019-04150-7.

   Whereas most studies indicate that an increase of power leads to an increase in unethical behavior, it seems the relationship between power and morality is more complex than that. For people who perceive themselves to be morally driven, more power can actually increase ethical behavior. See Joris Lammers et al., "Power and Morality," *Current Opinion in Psychology* 6 (December 2015): 15–19, https://doi.org/10.1016/j.copsyc.2015.03.018; Katherine A. DeCelles et al., "Does Power Corrupt or Enable? When and Why Power Facilitates Self-Interested Behavior," *Journal of Applied Psychology* 97, no. 3 (2012): 681–89, https://doi.org/10.1037/a0026811.

13. Gerben A. van Kleef et al., "Power, Distress, and Compassion: Turning a Blind Eye to the Suffering of Others," *Psychological Science* 19, no. 12 (December 2008): 1315–22, https://doi.org/10.1111/j.1467-9280.2008.02241.x.

14. The assertion that power is like a form of brain injury is based on an interview with Dacher Keltner. See Jerry Useem, "Power Causes Brain Damage," *The Atlantic*, July 2017, https://www.theatlantic.com/magazine/archive/2017/07/power-causes-brain-damage/528711/.

    Although this statement is hyperbolic, evidence suggests that feeling powerful reduces our brains' mirror neuron activity, making it neurologically harder to understand and empathize with others. See Jeremy Hogeveen, Michael Inzlicht, and Sukhvinder S. Obhi, "Power Changes How the Brain Responds to Others," *Journal of Experimental Psychology: General* 143, no. 2 (2014): 755–62, https://doi.org/10.1037/a0033477.

15. For a deeper look at formal and informal power as well as the important and dynamic role power plays in conflict, see Coleman's book: Peter T. Coleman and Robert Ferguson, *Making Conflict Work: Harnessing the Power of Disagreement* (Boston: Houghton Mifflin Harcourt, 2014).

16. Constantinos G. V. Coutifaris and Adam M. Grant, "Taking Your Team Behind the Curtain: The Effects of Leader Feedback-Sharing and Feedback-Seeking on Team Psychological Safety," *Organization Science* 33, no. 4 (July 2022): 1574–98, https://doi.org/10.1287/orsc.2021.1498.

17. Robin's story was inspired by a podcast interview with Tara Mac Aulay.

    Tara Mac Aulay, "How the Audacity to Fix Things without Asking Permission Can Change the World, Demonstrated by Tara Mac Aulay," interview by Robert Wiblin, June 22, 2018, *80,000 Hours*, podcast, audio and transcript, 1:22:34, https://80000hours.org/podcast/episodes/tara-mac-aulay-operations-mindset/.

18. Adam M. Grant, "Employees without a Cause: The Motivational Effects of Prosocial Impact in Public Service," *International Public Management Journal* 11, no. 1 (2008): 48–66, https://doi.org/10.1080/10967490801887905; Adam M. Grant et al., "Impact and the Art of Motivation Maintenance: The Effects of Contact with Beneficiaries on Persistence Behavior," *Organizational Behavior and Human Decision Processes* 103, no. 1 (May 2007): 53–67, https://doi.org/10.1016/j.obhdp.2006.05.004.

19. Judith M. Harackiewicz and Andrew J. Elliot, "The Joint Effects of Target and Purpose Goals on Intrinsic Motivation: A Mediational Analysis," *Personality and Social Psychology Bulletin* 24, no. 7 (July 1998): 675–89, https://doi.org/10.1177/0146167298247001. Although task-related goals can undermine intrinsic motivation, motivation grows when those tasks align with a broader purpose.

20. The idea of clear, up-to-date role descriptions and priorities is inspired by principles of Holacracy. Robertson, Brian J. *Holacracy: The New Management System for a Rapidly Changing World* (New York: Henry Holt, 2015).

21. Reverse dominance: Teasing appears to be a common feature of egalitarian societies, likely as a way to make sure that people with power maintain a sense of humility. Christopher Boehm et al., "Egalitarian Behavior and Reverse Dominance Hierarchy [and Comments and Reply]," *Current Anthropology* 34, no. 3 (June 1993): 227–54, https://doi.org/10.1086/204166.

22. A great deal of research illuminates the importance of autonomy (i.e., having a say in one's own work) to motivation. For an excellent theoretical and empirical approach to this topic, see Edward Deci and Richard Ryan's Self-Determination Theory: Delia O'Hara, "The

Intrinsic Motivation of Richard Ryan and Edward Deci," American Psychological Association, December 18, 2017, https://www.apa.org/members/content/intrinsic-motivation.

The following is a more recent examination of self-determination, autonomy, and control in the workplace: Jane X. Y. Chong and Marylène Gagné, "Self-Determination Theory for Work Motivation," in *Oxford Bibliographies in Management*, ed. R. Griffin, [chapter page range]. New York: Oxford University Press, 2019. http://dx.doi.org/10.1093/obo/9780199846740-0182.

23. For a review of Dweck's growth mindset research and theory, see Carol S. Dweck, *Mindset* (London: Constable & Robinson, 2012).

24. The skylight entrance is an example of an important concept known as *universal design*. It is the practice of designing spaces, systems, and products to be accessible to individuals with disabilities. Doing so not only creates a more inclusive society but also extends the benefits of these designs to people with more typical abilities and needs. Everyone benefits.

25. The concept of job crafting (i.e., adjusting one's work to better fit one's strengths and interests) was popularized by researchers Amy Wrzesniewski and Jane Dutton. Since then, a large body of research has pointed to the positive, lasting relationship between job crafting and engagement at work. Here's one example: Donald E. Frederick and Tyler J. VanderWeele, "Longitudinal Meta-Analysis of Job Crafting Shows Positive Association with Work Engagement," *Cogent Psychology* 7, no. 1 (April 17, 2020), https://doi.org/10.1080/23311908.2020.1746733.

26. For empirical evidence of the value of building over buying, consider research on the "IKEA Effect," which shows that people place a higher value on items they make than the very same items they did not.

Psychologists speculate that playing an active role in creating something increases our sense of ownership and attachment. See, for example, Michael I. Norton, Daniel Mochon, and Dan Ariely, "The 'IKEA Effect': When Labor Leads to Love" (working paper, Harvard Business School, 11-091, 2011), *SSRN Electronic Journal* https://doi.org/10.2139/ssrn.1777100.

27. For excellent guidance on leading change initiatives, see Chip Heath and Dan Heath, *Switch: How to Change Things When Change Is Hard* (New York: Currency, 2010); Alan Deutschman, *Change or Die: The Three Keys to Change at Work and in Life* (New York: HarperBusiness, 2007); John P. Kotter, *Leading Change* (Boston: Harvard Business Press, 2012).

    And if you'd like to learn about change by following another animal story, try John Kotter and Holger Rathgeber, *Our Iceberg Is Melting: Changing and Succeeding Under Any Conditions* (New York: Portfolio, 2016).

28. Google studied one hundred of its teams as part of its 2012 Project Aristotle to identify the behaviors of the most effective teams. It found that equal conversational turn-taking was one of the best predictors of high performance. For additional research on inclusive turn-taking, see Ki-Won Haan, Christoph Riedl, and Anita Woolley. "Discovering Where We Excel: How Inclusive Turn-Taking in Conversation Improves Team Performance," in *Companion Publication of the 2021 International Conference on Multimodal Interaction* (New York: ACM, 2021), 278–83, http://dx.doi.org/10.1145/3461615.3485417.

29. For further reading on psychological safety at work, see Amy C. Edmondson, *The Fearless Organization: Creating Psychological Safety in the Workplace for Learning, Innovation, and Growth* (Hoboken, NJ: John Wiley & Sons, 2018); Daniel Coyle, *The Culture Code: The Secrets of Highly Successful Groups* (New York: Bantam Books, 2018).

30. Alison Wood Brooks, Francesca Gino, and Maurice E. Schweitzer. "Smart People Ask for (My) Advice: Seeking Advice Boosts Perceptions of Competence." *Management Science* 61, no. 6 (June 2015): 1421–35. https://doi.org/10.1287/mnsc.2014.2054. Contrary to the common fear that seeking advice makes us seem incompetent, people tend to see us as *more* competent when we ask them for advice on tough topics.

••• INSIDER TESTIMONIALS •••

From time to time, I meet people who are skeptical about the feasibility of building a shared-power workplace. The best response I have to this concern is to encourage people to simply select a small power-with experiment to try for themselves. The second-best thing I can say is actually nothing but to let the people who have experienced it speak for themselves. I asked several former and current coworkers what it's like to be part of a power-with workplace. Here is what they had to say:

> "I've never felt more capable, trusted, and valued at work. One of the coolest outcomes of our power-with environment has been seeing great business ideas come from every department and *every level*. The results are a workplace of empowered humans who contribute more of their strengths to the business."
> —Robyn Long

> "Working in a power-with culture has connected me to my own strengths and ability to bring out the best in others. It's felt like a true teamwork environment without weird power struggles. I'd recommend it to anyone who's not afraid to challenge the status quo."
> —Megan Wheeler

"Simply put, a power-with approach is the end of alienation in the workplace—where people are removed from what they are creating—and the beginning of true cooperation. While it might not be perfect for every scenario (what method is?), changing conditions in the modern workplace call—nay, scream—for a new method of organization and operation. The power-with approach is undoubtedly the wave of the future."

—Roi Ben-Yehuda

"Working in a power-with environment feels like your colleagues are invested in your learning and success. It creates a broader sense of ownership across the company, which leads to more inclusive ways of working, and breeds resilience and community."

—Vanessa Tanicien

"Being part of a power-with workplace has increased my confidence in being a leader and helped me find a leadership style that feels authentic to me. I'd recommend it to any team or company that wants to continue to grow their employees and show them that leaders can be all types of people."

—Vim Dong

"Though I'm grateful for the experience and mentorship I received in hierarchical companies, the power-over structure can be disempowering because, despite your expertise, someone in a higher position can shoot down an idea without explanation. Working in a shared power environment is extremely empowering and rewarding. My thoughts and experiences are genuinely validated. Ultimately, this makes me work harder because there is shared responsibility for building our organization together. I'm not just a cog in a machine."

—Sharleen Benalvo

"What is the worst work environment you can think of? People are disrespectful. The rules of the game change regularly and without warning. No one knows how their work impacts the business or their colleagues. Your boss's mood dictates your quality of life. 'Power-with' creates simple organizational systems that discourage the things that get in the way of productive work and encourage employees to stick around and share their best ideas. I have no doubt most household name companies will deploy most of these practices in the next 10–20 years, and companies that adopt these practices early will have talent that produces a competitive advantage."

—Robleh Kirce

··· ACKNOWLEDGMENTS ···

So many brilliant and generous individuals played a role in bringing this book to life. Some of them even read (and reread) various drafts and gave me their thoughtful feedback. If you enjoyed this book, here are some of the people I have to thank for it:

Michael Campbell, my editor, thought partner, and squirrel-pun enabler who brought this book into existence and made it better every step of the way.

Brian Luna, my soulmate, playmate, coach, and the best teacher I could imagine for building a power-with relationship.

Alyssa Greene-Crow, my friend, feedback-giver, forever-neighbor, and partner in creating power-with workplaces through Scarlet Spark.

Roi Ben-Yehuda, who introduced me to Mary Parker Follett's writing and encouraged every one of my power-with experiments.

Paloma Medina, whose wise counsel and unwavering friendship have made everything from this book better and whose influence skills inspired the Paloma character in this book.

Thomas Wedell-Wedellsborg, for the most thorough and thoughtful editing a writer could ever dream of, along with endless soul resuscitation support.

Julie Foregerr, who's read just about everything I've ever written since we were teenagers and has made me a better writer, leader, and friend.

LeeAnn Renninger, who co-led so many power-with experiments at LifeLabs Learning and who (in her very Lee-Ann way) made this book more useful and more fun.

Olga Petrova, for raising me to be a skeptic and a rebel and for her willingness to read my drafts even when she didn't agree with my perspectives.

Amy Meng, for popping into my life just when I needed help with this book and inspiring me with her own workplace experiments.

Doug Stone, for his coaching, feedback, encouragement, songs, and much-needed reminders to keep my life and my writing fun.

Lisa Safran, the kind, creative oddball who cheered me on when I mentioned I might tell this story through squirrels and gave me the confidence to follow through.

Matthew Benedon, who loves animals and stories as much as I do and makes this world a kinder place.

Additional gratitude for book input goes to Ryan Foregerr, Leah Carey, Priscila Bala, Robleh Kirce, Xiao Ling, and Nathan Knight (whose ingenuity and love of squirrels inspired the squirrel who solves the Nuts for You crisis).

And many heartfelt thank-yous go to the following:

My eLab team, especially founders Sarah Holloway and Fernando Fabre, for working so hard to make the power of education accessible to all.

Our clients at LifeLabs Learning, who challenge the status quo to make their workplaces reflections of the power-with world they seek to build.

Our clients at Scarlet Spark, who don't just seek to share power with humans but also with all living beings so we can achieve true mutual flourishing.

My former CEO Vistage group, led by Jonathan Shapiro, whose vulnerability and generous mutual care are the opposite of the High Tails *nut*-work.

Speechify, a text-to-speech reader that helped my dyslexic brain read my own writing—sometimes even in the voice of Snoop Dogg.

The land I live on and the animals I live with, for your love and word-free wisdom (especially our pigs, Remi and JoJo, who sat beside me as I wrote and inspired the squirrel twins in the book).

··· BIOGRAPHIES ···

Tania Luna, Author
Tania is a psychology researcher, writer, and educator. She has built and grown multiple companies, including LifeLabs Learning, a leadership development resource that serves some of the world's most influential companies, and Scarlet Spark, a nonprofit that accelerates the speed-to-mission of organizations that help animals. Across her work, Tania strives to inspire interconnectedness among all living beings, humans included. She lives with rescued pigs, goats, roosters, dogs, cats, and the love of her life. For additional books and resources, head to www.TaniaLuna.com.

Process Grey, Illustrator
Father of three amazing humans. Artist and advocate for artists. Style is a medium, use with caution. Current toolbox: ink, digital, graphite, AI, paint. The illustrations created for this book used midjourney AI as a conceptual jumping-off point. The final result is a collage of a few AI concepts, built on with graphite and digital media. More examples of over twenty years of creation @process_grey Twitter / Instagram.